The Rooms Where Deals Still Happen

Published by Underwood Holdings, Birmingham, AL

The stories of Vanessa, Stacy, and other individuals depicted in this book are composite narratives drawn from the author's professional experience and research, including conversations with women across banking, finance, real estate, law, consulting, and entrepreneurship. Names, identifying details, and specific circumstances have been changed or fictionalized. The patterns described reflect documented research on professional networks, gender dynamics in business, and the role of informal environments in career advancement. Any resemblance to actual persons, living or deceased, is coincidental.

Case illustrations, statistics, and institutional examples throughout this book are intended for educational and analytical purposes. They do not constitute career, financial, legal, or business advice. Readers should consult qualified professionals regarding their specific circumstances.

ISBN: 978-1-953653-18-5

First Edition

Printed in the United States of America

THE ROOMS WHERE DEALS STILL HAPPEN

Why Golf, Relationships, and Access Will Outlast Algorithms

Shella Sylla

Underwood Holdings
Birmingham, Alabama

For the woman who knows she belongs in the room, but hasn't always been invited.

For the professional ready to be seen, trusted, and chosen.

For the entrepreneur who understands that access is the real currency.

And for those willing to step onto the course to claim it.

This book is your playbook for using golf, relationships, and proximity to open doors, build influence, and create opportunities that algorithms never will.

Acknowledgements

This journey did not happen alone.

To my parents, thank you for the foundation you gave me. Your values, your sacrifices, and your belief in what is possible have shaped everything I am building today.

To my siblings, thank you for your constant support, encouragement, and presence along the way.

A special thank you to my sister, Martha. You encouraged me to bring SisterGolf to Birmingham, Alabama at a time when it was just an idea. Your belief helped turn vision into action.

To Kevin Alston, an avid golfer and a friend I met in Charlotte, thank you for pushing me. After hearing about SisterGolf, you didn't just support the idea, you insisted that I build it. That insistence mattered more than you know.

To Bob Marshall, a fellow Charlotte friend and golfer who shared my love for the game and understood its power. When I moved to Birmingham and began building SisterGolf, Bob never lost touch. He would check in and offer encouragement, especially in the early days when I needed it most. That steady, quiet belief made a difference I will never forget.

To the early supporters in Birmingham who said yes before there was proof:

Marcella Roberts

Annie Allen

Darlene Wilson Gallien

Tracy Morant Adams

Matt Jones

Candace Schepperle

Natalie Holland

Bob Dickerson

Thank you for trusting the vision and helping lay the foundation.

To every woman who has ever been a member of SisterGolf, attended an event, participated in a workshop, or taken a lesson: you are the reason this exists. SisterGolf was built for you, but it continues because of you.

To Brandon Mason and 3BM Golf Studio, thank you for your partnership, your expertise, and your commitment to helping our members grow in the game.

To Ed Fields and Mayor Randall Woodfin, thank you for your leadership and your support of initiatives that create access, opportunity, and community through the game of golf.

There are many others who have contributed to this journey in ways both big and small. If your name is not listed here, please know that your impact has not been overlooked. It has been felt, and it is appreciated.

Contents

INTRODUCTION

The Secret Nobody Told Us

I was working harder than anyone in my office.

I know that sounds like something everyone says, but I mean it literally. I was the first one in and often one of the last to leave. I had studied. I had trained. I had taken every sales course my employer offered, sat in every seminar, and absorbed every framework they put in front of me. I was doing everything right, at least everything I had been told to do.

And I was still falling behind.

Meanwhile, something strange was happening around me. My male colleagues, some of whom I knew for a fact were not working as hard, not as polished in a client meeting, not as sharp on the details, were hitting their numbers. Exceeding them, even. Month after month. And then, seemingly out of nowhere, they'd duck out of the office early on a Thursday afternoon, laughing and loose, golf bags slung over their shoulders.

I didn't understand it at first. I told myself it was politics. I told myself it was bias, which honestly wasn't entirely wrong. I told myself a lot of things that let me stay comfortable in my frustration instead of curious about what was actually happening.

Then one day, a male colleague pulled me aside. Not in a formal mentoring kind of way, but in the way a friend whispers something useful across a dinner table. He told me the truth. The relationships that were driving business weren't being built in conference rooms or over email threads. They were being built on golf courses. At charity tournaments. Over four hours of walking eighteen holes where, somewhere between the fourth and the fourteenth, people stopped being colleagues and started being people who trusted each other.

That was the moment everything changed for me.

I want to be clear about what that moment felt like: it wasn't empowering. Not immediately. It was actually a little infuriating. Because if golf was where the real business was happening, and women weren't in those spaces, weren't invited, weren't prepared, didn't know what they were missing, then we weren't just losing ground on the scorecard. We were losing ground in the economy. Deal by deal. Promotion by promotion. Partnership by partnership.

I decided to do something about it.

I signed up for golf lessons. I recruited two of my girlfriends to take lessons with me, because that's how we do things. We don't go into uncomfortable territory alone if we can help it. I practiced. I showed up to a company charity tournament as the only woman in a field of one hundred men, played terribly, and had the most professionally productive day of my career up to that point.

Not because I made any incredible shots. I didn't.

But because I was *there.* I knew how to participate. I could speak the language. And in that environment, four hours, no phones, no agendas, no performance reviews, I connected with people who became my biggest referral sources. Within months, I went from struggling to hit my $500,000 monthly production goal to becoming a repeat member of the Million Dollar Club, a designation reserved for associates who exceeded one million dollars in production in a single month.

Golf didn't make me better at banking. It made me visible to the people who could send business my way. That is a fundamentally different thing, and it is the lesson this entire book is built around.

What This Book Is and Who It's For

This is not a golf instruction book. I am not going to teach you how to fix your swing or improve your short game. There are plenty of books and coaches for that, and frankly, your handicap is not the point.

This is a book about access. About the invisible economy of relationships that quietly drives who gets the client, who gets the promotion, who gets the deal, who gets considered. It is a book about the environments where that economy operates and how to intentionally position yourself inside them.

Golf is the lens. But the vision is much wider.

This book is for two kinds of women.

The first is the woman building influence inside an organization. She has put in the work. She has the credentials, the competence, the track record. And she is watching people with less experience and, if she's honest with herself, less talent, get ahead of her. She suspects, or perhaps she knows, that something is happening in conversations she is not part of. She is right.

The second is the woman building something of her own. The entrepreneur, the consultant, the founder, the business owner who knows that the difference between a business that struggles and a business that scales often comes down to who knows you, who trusts you, and who picks up the phone when you call. She is not waiting for a corporate ladder. She is building her own structure. But she still needs the same things: clients, capital, partners, referrals, visibility in the rooms where decisions are made.

Both women need access to the same networks. Both benefit from the same relationship ecosystems. Both gain real, measurable power when they learn how to enter the rooms where opportunities originate.

Access is not a personality trait. It is a practice. And it is learnable.

There is something happening in the professional world that makes this conversation more urgent than it has ever been.

Artificial intelligence is transforming the workplace at a pace none of us have fully come to terms with. Tasks that once required years of training are being automated. Roles that once represented job security are being restructured or eliminated. The professional landscape that many of us built our careers inside is being renegotiated in real time, and the professionals who will thrive in what comes next are not necessarily the ones with the most technical skills.

They are the ones who cannot be replaced by a prompt.

What AI cannot do is build trust. As automation makes technical competence more common and less differentiating, the value of genuine human connection goes up, not down. The rooms where deals still happen become more valuable, not less. We will go much deeper on that argument in Chapter 9. For now, understand this: the professionals who will thrive in the next decade are not the ones who compete with algorithms. They are the ones who invest in something algorithms cannot replicate.

This is not a reason to ignore technology. It is a reason to invest just as seriously in your relationship capital as you do in your professional skills.

The Idea That Wouldn't Leave

I first had the idea for SisterGolf in 2003. I want to sit with that date for a second, because it matters to the story.

I didn't launch it until 2013. Ten years later.

I tried. While I was still in banking, I started talking about the concept, testing the waters, trying to get women interested in the idea that golf could change their professional trajectories. The reception was lukewarm at best. Women didn't see golf as relevant to their careers. It felt like a hobby, something men did, something that would require them to be embarrassed and incompetent in front of people whose opinions mattered. The timing wasn't right, the culture wasn't ready, and honestly, I didn't yet have the full bandwidth to build something from scratch while also doing my day job.

Then the housing crash of 2008 came. A former commercial real estate client became my business partner, and together we took the leap, left corporate America, and opened an independent financial advisory firm in Charlotte, North Carolina. It was my first real taste of entrepreneurship, and it confirmed something I had suspected for years: that building something of your own requires a completely different set of muscles than excelling inside someone else's institution. Charlotte gave me the courage to bet on myself. But it also made clear that the city wasn't where I was supposed to be.

My sister was in Birmingham. She had been encouraging me for years to come, to finally build SisterGolf for real, in a place where she believed the community would receive it. So I went. I gave myself eighteen months. I fully expected to not like it, but Birmingham surprised me and won me over.

The idea stayed with me through every detour and transition. It didn't fade. It didn't become less urgent. If anything, the years of watching talented women remain invisible while men leveraged access and relationships made the mission feel more necessary, not less.

There is a quote I return to often: *If you have a business idea and years go by and it does not leave you, then you know it is something you have to pursue.* That was SisterGolf for me. Ten years of not being able to let it go.

Birmingham's ecosystem for entrepreneurs, the warmth, the access, the community of people genuinely invested in watching you succeed, was unlike anything I had experienced in larger markets. It became the fuel. SisterGolf found its footing and has been growing ever since.

What Changed and What Hasn't

When I first started talking about business golf for women, the conversation was hard. Women were intimidated by the sport, unsure they'd be welcomed, unconvinced the connection between a golf round and a business outcome was real.

Then something shifted in the culture.

TopGolf arrived and removed the most significant barrier to entry: the fear of embarrassment on a traditional course. Suddenly women could pick up a club in a social, forgiving environment where the point was fun first and skill second. The psychological weight of "I don't know how to play" got lighter. Women started having the conversation.

And then pop culture got involved. Celebrity women started going public about their love of golf. The game stopped feeling like an old boys' club and started feeling like something powerful women did on purpose. That visibility matters. It always has. When women can see themselves in a space, they start to believe they belong there.

But here is what hasn't changed: the boardrooms and golf courses and private dinners and charity tournaments where relationships form and deals originate are still, overwhelmingly, places where women remain underrepresented. The access gap is smaller than it was. The awareness gap has narrowed considerably. But the opportunity gap, the gap between who is in those rooms and who could benefit from being there, is still enormous.

That is exactly why this book exists.

One Last Thing Before We Begin

You do not need to become a golfer to benefit from what follows. You need to become someone who understands relationship capital: what it is, how it is built, and how to position yourself in the environments where it accumulates. Golf is the lens. The vision is much wider.

By the time you finish, you will not look at a golf invitation, a dinner, a conference, a charity event, or any gathering where decision-makers are present the same way again. That is not a promise about golf. It is a promise about how you see opportunity, and who controls access to it.

Let's get into the rooms.

"If you can find your ball, you're still in the game."

CHAPTER ONE

The Day the Ladder Started Disappearing

You already know part of what comes next. The rooms exist. The question is why, and what it costs when you are not in them.

There is a story we were all told about how success works.

You work hard. You develop expertise. You perform well. You get noticed, get promoted, get rewarded. The ladder is there. You climb it. The formula is linear, logical, and if you are a woman who has spent any time in a serious professional environment, you have probably already figured out that it does not quite work the way it was described.

The ladder was never as reliable as advertised. But something has happened in the last decade that has made the gap between the story and the reality even wider, even harder to ignore.

The ladder is disappearing.

Not metaphorically. Structurally. The organizational architecture that created predictable paths from entry-level to senior management to executive leadership is being compressed, automated, and fundamentally restructured. Companies are flatter. Hierarchies are thinner. The middle management layers that once served as both stepping stones and training grounds are being eliminated at a rate that should be alarming to anyone who assumed those rungs would still be there when they needed them.

Understanding why this is happening, and what it means for how you build a career or a business, is the foundation of everything that follows in this book.

The Great Compression

For most of the twentieth century, large organizations were built vertically. There were many layers between the person answering the phones and the person running the company, and each layer represented a career milestone: a promotion, a raise, a new title, a new set of responsibilities. The structure was bureaucratic, occasionally infuriating, but it was also legible. You knew where you were. You knew where you were trying to go. You knew roughly what it would take to get there.

That structure served companies, too. Middle managers coordinated information, supervised teams, made decisions that didn't need executive attention, and created the organizational connective tissue that kept large institutions functioning. They were expensive, but they were necessary.

Then came technology. Then came the internet. Then came enterprise software that could coordinate, track, analyze, and report in ways that previously required entire departments of human beings. And then came artificial intelligence, which didn't just automate individual tasks but began to replace entire categories of cognitive work, analysis, synthesis, communication, problem-solving, that middle management was largely built around.

The result is what organizational researchers are now calling the Great Compression: a rapid flattening of corporate hierarchies as companies realize they can operate effectively with far fewer management layers than they once needed. McKinsey estimates that generative AI could automate up to 70 percent of the tasks currently performed by knowledge workers. Not 70 percent of jobs, but 70 percent of the *tasks* that make up those jobs. The distinction sounds reassuring until you realize what it means in practice: that the value of showing up and doing the work, reliably and competently, has been fundamentally repriced.

This is not a prediction about the future. It is a description of the present.

What Happens When Competence Becomes a Commodity

Here is the uncomfortable truth at the center of this chapter: in a world where AI can perform an increasing share of the tasks that used to define professional value, competence alone is no longer enough to differentiate you.

It never fully was, if we are being honest. But the gap between the story we were told and the reality we are living in has never been wider.

Think about what used to make someone valuable in a professional context. Knowledge: the accumulated expertise that took years to develop and couldn't be quickly replicated. Analytical ability: the capacity to take complex information and synthesize it into something actionable. Communication skills: the ability to write clearly, present persuasively, explain complicated things in simple terms. These were real differentiators. They were and still are things that, increasingly, a well-prompted AI system can do in seconds.

This is not an argument against developing skills. Skills still matter. Expertise still matters. Being genuinely good at what you do is still table stakes, a necessary but no longer sufficient condition for professional success.

What becomes rare, what becomes genuinely scarce and therefore genuinely valuable, is something that no algorithm can produce: the trust of another human being.

Trust is not transferable. It is not scalable. It cannot be automated, outsourced, or purchased. It is built in the slow, inefficient, deeply human process of spending time with people, showing them who you are, demonstrating consistency between what you say and what you do, and creating the kind of relationship where they would stake something of value, a referral, a recommendation, a contract, a partnership, on their belief in you.

In an economy where tasks are increasingly cheap, trust is increasingly expensive. And the people who understand how to build it, strategically, intentionally, at scale, will be the ones who win.

The Power Funnel

I want to introduce a concept here that will recur throughout this book: the power funnel.

The old professional model was shaped like a pyramid. Many people entered at the base. Through a combination of performance and tenure, a portion advanced to middle levels. A smaller portion reached senior levels. A very small number reached the top. It was a wide pyramid and there were paths.

The new model is shaped more like a funnel. The opening is still wide. But the passage narrows much more quickly, and the narrowing is no longer governed primarily by performance. It is governed by visibility and connection.

Here is what this means in practice: two professionals with identical skill sets, identical education, identical track records, and identical ambitions will have dramatically different outcomes based on a single variable. Who knows them, and who vouches for them, in the rooms where decisions are made.

The person who gets the promotion is not always the most qualified person for the job. The person who wins the client is not always the person who submitted the best proposal. The person who closes the deal is not always the one with the most expertise. They are, reliably and consistently, the person who had the relationship, the one who existed in the decision-maker's mind before the decision was being made.

This is not cynicism. This is not an argument that merit doesn't matter. It is an honest accounting of how professional opportunity actually flows. And if you are going to navigate this new landscape, whether you are building a career inside an organization or building a business of your own, you need to understand the terrain you are actually operating in, not the one you were told to expect.

The Women Who Saw This Coming

There is a particular kind of pain that belongs to women who are highly competent in male-dominated industries.

It is the pain of watching less qualified people move past you. Of sitting in meetings where your idea gets dismissed and then praised when a male colleague says the same thing fifteen minutes later. Of doing the work, hitting the numbers, earning the credentials, and still feeling like you are pressing your face against glass, watching opportunities form and flow on the other side.

I have sat in that frustration. I have felt that particular combination of exhaustion and confusion that comes from doing everything right and still somehow being overlooked.

What I eventually understood, and what took me longer than I wish it had, is that the problem wasn't my performance. It was my positioning.

The people who were advancing, who were winning clients, who were being promoted and celebrated and referred and included, were not necessarily working harder or thinking more clearly. They were simply operating in a different ecosystem. They had access to environments where trust was built, where relationships deepened, where informal conversations led to formal opportunities. They were inside the funnel.

And most women, through a combination of exclusion, unfamiliarity, and not understanding what they were missing, were and still are outside of it.

Here is what changes when you understand this: you stop trying to fix things that aren't broken. You stop working harder on the things you are already doing well. You start asking a different question entirely.

Not "What do I need to do better?" but "Where do I need to be?"

The New Currency

The professionals who will thrive in the next decade, the ones who will be opportunity-rich while others become invisible, are the ones who have built what I call *relationship capital.*

Relationship capital is not your network. A network is a list of people you could theoretically contact. Relationship capital is something more specific and more valuable: the accumulated trust, goodwill, and visibility you hold in the minds of people who are positioned to either create opportunities themselves or connect you to the people who can.

It has four components, and we will build on each of them throughout this book:

Access: your presence in the environments where relationships form and decisions are made.

Visibility: the degree to which the right people know who you are, what you stand for, and what you are capable of.

Trust: the belief, held by people who matter to your goals, that you are reliable, credible, and worth vouching for.

Opportunity Flow: the ongoing stream of introductions, referrals, conversations, and invitations that result when the first three are in place.

Most professionals focus on visibility alone, building a brand, posting content, attending events, accumulating connections. These things matter. But visibility without access means being seen from a distance. Visibility without trust means being known but not believed. And trust without opportunity flow means having a strong reputation that isn't translating into anything tangible.

Relationship capital is the full system. And building it requires being intentional about where you spend your time, who you spend it with, and what environments you put yourself inside.

The Rooms Are Still There

Here is the thing about the professional landscape being reshaped by technology: it has changed almost everything about how work is done, and almost nothing about where the most consequential relationships are formed.

The rooms where deals still happen are not in your inbox. They are not on a Zoom call, however well-produced. They are in the physical environments where people gather without an agenda, where the conversation has space to breathe, where the relationship can develop at the pace relationships actually develop at, where trust accumulates not in a single exchange but over the course of an afternoon.

Golf courses. Private dinners. Charity tournaments. Conferences and retreats. The spaces that exist at the intersection of professional purpose and genuine human connection.

These environments have existed for as long as commerce has existed, and they have survived every wave of technological disruption that was supposed to make them obsolete. They survived the fax machine and the conference call and the email revolution and the rise of social media. They will survive artificial intelligence too, not because they are nostalgic or because the people who use them are resistant to change, but because they serve a function that technology has never been able to replicate.

They give people the time and space to decide whether they trust each other.

That function will not become obsolete. It will become more valuable.

The question is not whether the rooms still matter. They do. The question is whether you are in them.

What This Means for You

Here is what I need you to hear before we go any further.

If you are reading this and you have been working hard, doing good work, and still feeling stuck, I want you to consider the possibility that the problem is not your performance. The problem may be your positioning. You may be optimizing for a game that has changed, investing in a currency that has been devalued, climbing a ladder that is shorter than it used to be.

The path forward is not to work harder on the things you are already doing. The path forward is to add something to your professional strategy that most of your competitors, male or female, have not fully understood yet.

It is to build your relationship capital with the same intention and discipline that you bring to everything else.

And one of the most powerful environments for doing that, one with a documented history of generating exactly the kind of trust and access and opportunity flow that moves careers and grows businesses, happens to involve a small white ball, eighteen holes, and four hours away from your desk.

Relationship capital is the new competitive advantage. The chapters ahead show you how to build it.

"Competence opens the door. But it is relationship capital that decides who walks through."

CHAPTER TWO

Why Skills Alone Are No Longer Enough

Meet Vanessa.

Vanessa is thirty-eight years old, fourteen years into a career in commercial real estate finance. She has an MBA from a well-regarded university. She has closed deals that most of her peers haven't been trusted with yet. She consistently receives strong performance reviews. Her clients like her. Her manager respects her. By every measurable standard, she is exactly the kind of professional her company should be fighting to keep and promote.

She has been passed over for senior vice president twice.

The first time, she was told the timing wasn't right. There would be other opportunities. She accepted that, went back to her desk, and worked harder. She took on more accounts. She stayed later. She volunteered for the projects nobody else wanted. She made herself indispensable in every way she knew how.

The second time, the role went to a colleague with two fewer years of experience, a thinner book of business, and, as far as Vanessa could tell, no obvious advantage over her except one: he played golf every other Friday with the regional managing director.

Vanessa is a composite, drawn from dozens of real conversations with real women. Her story is not fictional. It is one of the most common stories I hear from women in professional services, finance, technology, real estate, and corporate America broadly. I changed the specifics to protect the people involved. The frustration, the pattern, the outcome: those are unchanged.

What happened to Vanessa is not primarily a story about gender bias, though bias is certainly part of the picture. It is a story about a fundamental misunderstanding of how professional advancement actually works. And until we name that misunderstanding clearly, we cannot fix it.

The Meritocracy Myth

We were told a story about meritocracy, and most of us believed it because it was the only story on offer.

Work hard. Develop skills. Produce results. Get rewarded. The logic was clean and reassuring. It suggested that professional success was a function of what you could do, and that what you could do was something you could control. Study more. Practice more. Deliver more. The formula was yours to execute.

The problem is that meritocracy, as a system, requires someone to evaluate merit. And that evaluation does not happen in a vacuum. It happens in the minds of human beings who have limited time, limited information, and a deeply human tendency to favor the people who look like them, think like them, move through the world like them.

Corporate America is not a meritocracy. It is a mirror-tocracy.

People promote the people who remind them of themselves. They sponsor the colleagues who feel familiar. They advocate in rooms you're not in for the people they've broken bread with, shared a round of golf with, sat next to at a conference dinner. It is not always conscious. It is not always malicious. But it is consistent, and it is documented, and if you have ever watched a less qualified person advance past you and wondered what you were missing, the mirror is a large part of the answer.

Research on hiring and promotion decisions consistently shows that personal familiarity and trusted recommendations carry more weight than objective qualifications. A Harvard Business Review study found that up to 70 percent of jobs are filled through networking, meaning through relationships that existed before a formal process began. McKinsey's Women in the Workplace report has documented for years that women are held to higher performance standards than men for equivalent roles, yet still advance more slowly. The gap is not explained by performance. It is explained by visibility and sponsorship, which are themselves products of relationship access.

The meritocracy myth is not just inaccurate. It is actively harmful to the people who believe it most completely, because it causes them to invest more and more energy in the variable they can control, their skills and their output, while remaining blind to the variable that is actually driving decisions: their relationships.

The Room Where It Happens

If you know the musical Hamilton, you know the song. Aaron Burr watches Alexander Hamilton disappear into a closed-door meeting with James Madison and Thomas Jefferson, and the song that follows is his anguished, electric recognition of what has just happened: the most consequential decisions are being made in a room he is not in, by people he is not close enough to, about a future he has no voice in shaping.

"I want to be in the room where it happens," Burr sings. Not the room where the announcement is made. Not the room where the plan is executed. The room where the decision is born, where the deal is struck, where the relationship between power and opportunity becomes something real and binding.

That song, written about the founding of a nation, describes something that plays out every day in boardrooms, golf courses, private dinners, and charity tournaments across America. The deals, the promotions, the partnerships, the board appointments: they are shaped in informal spaces, between people who trust each other, long before they ever appear on a formal agenda.

The difference between Burr and Hamilton in that story is not talent. Hamilton was not obviously more gifted. The difference was access, and Hamilton's relentless willingness to put himself in every room he could find his way into.

Getting into the room. And knowing what to do once you're there. That is the work ahead.

Working Twice as Hard for Half the Credit

There is a particular version of this trap that belongs specifically to women, and even more specifically to women of color.

"Work twice as hard to get half the credit." It is advice passed down through generations, offered with genuine love by parents and mentors who understood something real about the world their daughters and mentees were entering. The implication was clear: the system is not fair, so you need to outperform the standard just to be seen as meeting it.

The advice was not wrong, exactly. It reflected a real and documented dynamic. But it had an unintended consequence: it trained generations of talented women to put all of their energy into performance, into the work itself, and to treat relationship-building, visibility, and strategic positioning as secondary concerns. Soft skills, they called it. Nice-to-haves. Things you did after the real work was done.

I felt this in my own career. I was raised to believe that excellence was its own argument. That if I was good enough, diligent enough, prepared enough, the results would speak for themselves. And they did speak. They just weren't being heard by the people who needed to hear them, because those people were having conversations I wasn't part of.

The cost of that belief is not theoretical. It shows up in compensation data, in promotion rates, in the persistent gap between women's qualifications and women's advancement. It shows up in the particular exhaustion of being undeniably good at your job and still feeling like you are fighting for a seat at a table that keeps getting moved.

Here is the reframe that changes everything: working harder is not the answer when the problem is not about your work. The answer is working differently. Specifically, it is building the relationships and visibility that make your excellent work visible to the people who control the outcomes you are working toward.

The Entrepreneur's Version of the Same Problem

I want to be careful not to let this chapter speak only to the corporate professional, because the entrepreneur faces an almost identical challenge, just wearing different clothes.

If you have ever built something, you know the particular heartbreak of a great product that nobody buys. Of a service that solves a real problem for the clients who find you, while dozens of potential clients who need exactly what you offer never find you at all. Of watching competitors with inferior offerings win contracts, attract investment, and grow their businesses while you wonder what they know that you don't.

What they often know, or what they have stumbled into without fully understanding it, is relationship capital.

Business does not grow primarily through advertising or content or cold outreach, though all of those things have their place. Business grows through trust. Through referrals from people who know you and believe in what you do. Through partnerships forged in environments where two people had enough time together to discover they were aligned. Through investors who backed a founder they believed in before they fully believed in the business plan.

The same invisible economy that governs corporate advancement governs entrepreneurial growth. The same access gap that holds back the corporate professional holds back the founder. And the same solution, intentional, strategic presence in the environments where trust is built and opportunity flows, applies in both contexts.

The woman who understands this, whether she is building influence inside an organization or building a business from scratch, has a fundamental advantage over the woman who is still trying to win on performance alone.

What Visibility Actually Means

We have all heard the phrase: it's not what you know, it's who you know.

It sounds true. And it is, as far as it goes. But it doesn't go far enough. Because in my experience, the real determining factor in professional opportunity is not who you know. It is who knows you, and what they are saying about you when you are not in the room.

That distinction is everything.

You can know the right people. You can have their contact information, their business cards, their connection on LinkedIn. But if they don't truly know you, if you are not alive in their minds as someone specific and credible and trustworthy, that connection is worth almost nothing when the moment of decision arrives.

Think about how real professional opportunities actually move. Someone is sitting across a dinner table and the conversation turns to a business problem. Someone else says, "You know who you should talk to?" A name comes up. Not because that person submitted a proposal or responded to a job posting. Because they were already in the room, in the mind, in the conversation, before the need was even fully articulated.

That is visibility in its most powerful form. Not a brand. Not a following. Not a title on a business card. It is being the name that comes up in the conversation you were not part of, spoken with confidence and genuine endorsement by someone whose opinion the decision-maker trusts.

Building that kind of visibility requires something that cannot be manufactured from a distance. It requires presence in the environments where those conversations happen, where the trust that produces endorsements is built, where people move from knowing your name to knowing your character.

Visibility does not mean being loud. It does not mean self-promotion in the uncomfortable, performative sense that makes many high-achievers cringe. It means being genuinely, memorably present with the people who matter, before you need anything from them, in contexts where they can see who you really are.

The golf course is one of the most effective environments ever invented for building exactly that kind of visibility. Four uninterrupted hours. No performance review. No agenda beyond the round itself. Just two or three or four people walking the same ground, facing the same small frustrations and occasional small triumphs, finding out over the course of eighteen holes whether they actually like each other.

That is where the real visibility is built. That is where we are going.

The Positioning Shift

Vanessa, whose story opened this chapter, eventually made a decision that changed her trajectory. Not a decision to work harder, though she was already working harder than almost anyone around her. A decision to change where she spent her time and who she spent it with.

She started saying yes to things she had previously declined: the Friday afternoon golf outing, the charity tournament her firm sponsored, the informal dinners after industry conferences that she used to skip in favor of getting back to the hotel to prepare for the next day's meetings.

She wasn't immediately comfortable. She didn't know how to play golf, and the first time she showed up to a company outing, she felt out of place and underprepared. But she was there. And being there, it turned out, was most of the work.

Within eight months, she had been introduced to three potential clients through relationships she built in those informal environments. One of them became her largest account. And the next time a senior vice president role opened at her firm, the regional managing director, the same one who had been playing golf every other Friday with her colleague, called her directly to tell her she was his recommendation.

She hadn't changed her skills. She had changed her positioning.

That is the shift this book is designed to help you make.

The Four Gaps

Based on years of working with women professionals across industries, I have identified four gaps that consistently hold talented women back. They are not gaps in competence. They are gaps in the four components of relationship capital: access, visibility, trust, and opportunity flow.

The *access gap* is the most fundamental. If you are not present in the environments where relationships form and decisions are made, none of the other variables can work in your favor. You cannot build visibility with people you never encounter. You cannot build trust with people who don't know you exist.

The *visibility gap* is what Vanessa experienced. She existed in the organization, but she did not exist in the minds of the people who controlled her advancement. Her excellent work was known to the people she worked with directly. It was not known, in any felt or personal way, to the people above her.

The *trust gap* is subtler and often the most painful, because it is the gap that high performers feel most acutely as a form of injustice. Trust, in professional environments, is built through familiarity as much as through demonstrated competence. People trust who they know. They promote who they trust. And they know best the people they have spent informal time with.

The *opportunity flow gap* is the downstream consequence of the first three. When you lack access, visibility, and trust with the right people, opportunities don't find their way to you. The referrals go elsewhere. The introductions happen in conversations you're not part of. The deals get done on courses you're not playing.

Closing these gaps is not a one-time event. It is a strategic, ongoing practice. And the chapters that follow are designed to give you the specific tools, environments, and frameworks to start closing them immediately.

A New Question

Before we move into the heart of the book, here is the reframe that changes everything.

Most ambitious professionals spend most of their energy on a single question: How do I get better at what I do?

It is a good question. It is not the only question, and for many high-achievers, it is no longer the most important one.

The question that changes trajectories is this: Who needs to know what I can do, and how do I make sure they know it in a way that builds trust rather than just awareness?

That question leads you somewhere different. It leads you away from your desk and into the environments where the people who matter are spending their informal time. It leads you to a golf course, to a charity scramble, to the drinks after work that you used to skip, to the industry dinner where the real conversations happen after the program ends, to the conference hallway where the connections outlast the sessions.

It leads you into the rooms. Let's go.

"Golf is not about how well you play. It is about who you play with and what happens between the shots."

CHAPTER THREE

The Hidden Economy of Relationships

There are two economies operating simultaneously in every professional environment, whether you are building a career inside an organization or building a business of your own.

The first is the visible one. Job postings, performance reviews, quarterly targets, org charts, compensation bands, promotion criteria. Sales funnels, marketing budgets, pitch decks, client proposals. This is the economy most professionals spend most of their time thinking about, planning around, and trying to optimize for. It is the economy with rules you can read, metrics you can measure, and progress you can track on a spreadsheet.

The second economy is invisible. It has no org chart and no written rules. It does not appear in any employee handbook or strategic plan, any business plan or marketing strategy. But it is, in most organizations and industries, the economy that actually determines who advances, who wins the client, who gets considered for the opportunity that never gets posted publicly, and who receives the kind of sponsorship that moves a career from competent to consequential.

This second economy runs on a single currency: relationship capital.

Understanding how it works, how opportunities actually originate and flow through professional networks, is the difference between spending your career optimizing for the wrong game and finally playing the one that actually counts.

How Opportunities Actually Move

Most people imagine professional opportunity flowing through formal channels. A position opens. It gets posted. Candidates apply. The best candidate gets selected. The process is clean, documented, fair.

This is not how most meaningful opportunities actually work.

Think about the last significant opportunity in your career or business. Not a routine assignment or a standard client engagement. A real inflection point: a promotion that changed your trajectory, a client that transformed your business, a partnership that opened doors you didn't know existed, a board appointment or speaking engagement or investment that shifted your professional standing.

Now ask yourself honestly: how did that opportunity actually find you?

In most cases, if you trace it back carefully, there is a relationship at the root. Someone mentioned your name.

Someone made an introduction. Someone said, "You should talk to her," in a conversation you were not part of, and that endorsement carried enough weight to open a door that formal processes would never have opened as quickly or as warmly.

This is not anecdotal. Research on professional mobility consistently shows that the majority of senior-level opportunities are filled through networks rather than formal processes, that sponsored candidates advance faster than equally qualified unsponsored ones, and that the single most reliable predictor of entrepreneurial success is not the quality of the product or the size of the market but the strength and reach of the founder's relationship network.

The hidden economy is real. It is large. And it is the primary driver of professional outcomes for people at every level, in every industry, whether they know it or not.

The Anatomy of a Real Opportunity

Think about how most meaningful professional opportunities actually arrive. Not through a job posting. Not through a performance review. Through a conversation that happened in a room you were or were not in.

Consider something I have watched happen dozens of times across industries and career levels. Two professionals, equally qualified, both strong performers, both wanting the same opportunity. Call them Lisa and Janet. Same company, same tenure, similar track records. Lisa spends her Friday afternoons at her desk, finishing work, staying visible in the ways she was taught to stay visible. Janet has played golf with the senior partners a handful of times. She is not invited every week. It is still very much a male-dominated space, and she knows that. But she has made herself enough of a known presence in those settings that when the partners do include others, her name comes up. She has played with them enough to be someone they know outside a conference room.

Lisa has a cleaner inbox. Janet has a relationship.

When the opportunity opens, Lisa is a name on a list. Janet is someone they already know.

Guess which one gets the call.

This is not about golf specifically, not yet. It is about the structure of how opportunity moves. The hidden economy does not reward the most qualified person. It rewards the most present one, in the right environment, at the right moment, with the right people. Qualification gets you into consideration. Relationship capital determines the outcome.

Relationship Capital: The Framework

Relationship capital is the accumulated trust, visibility, and goodwill you hold in the minds of people who are positioned to affect your professional outcomes. It is not your network. A network is structural, a list of connections. Relationship capital is experiential: it is the quality of what those connections actually think and feel about you, and the degree to which they are inclined to act on your behalf.

It is built through four interconnected components:

Access is the entry point. You cannot build relationship capital with people you never encounter. Access means being physically and socially present in the environments where the people who matter to your goals spend their informal time. A golf course is an access environment. So is a charity dinner, a conference, a mastermind group, a private club. Access is not about knowing the right people. It is about being in the right places.

Visibility is what happens when you have access and you use it well. Visibility is not about being seen. It is about being remembered, specifically and positively, by the people whose judgment shapes opportunities. The kind of visibility that moves careers is not broadcast visibility, it is relational visibility: you are the person who comes to mind when a trusted contact is asked for a recommendation.

Trust is the engine. Everything else in the relationship capital framework depends on trust. Trust is built through consistency, through demonstrated competence in low-stakes environments, through the accumulation of small interactions over time that add up to a reliable picture of who you are. You cannot manufacture trust quickly. You can, however, create the conditions under which it forms naturally, and informal environments like golf courses are specifically designed for exactly that.

Opportunity Flow is the output. When access, visibility, and trust are all functioning together, opportunities find you. Not randomly, but through the deliberate mechanics of a network that has been built with intention. Referrals come to you. Introductions get made. Your name comes up in the conversation you weren't part of.

This is not luck. This is a system. And like any system, it can be understood, built, and optimized.

The Compound Interest of Relationships

Here is something that most professionals don't fully appreciate about relationship capital: it compounds.

Financial capital compounds because returns generate additional returns over time. Relationship capital works the same way, except the returns are measured in trust and opportunity rather than dollars.

Every relationship you invest in has the potential to connect you to three or four others. Every person who trusts you enough to make an introduction extends your reach exponentially. Every opportunity that comes through your network, when handled with excellence and integrity, deepens existing relationships and creates new ones. The person who connected you to the opportunity becomes a stronger advocate. The person you helped with the opportunity becomes a new node in your network.

Over time, this compounding effect creates something that looks, from the outside, like luck. The professional who always seems to be in the right place at the right time, who always knows the right person, who always has a pipeline of interesting opportunities. What looks like luck is almost always the mature return on a long-term investment in relationship capital.

The challenge is that relationship capital, like financial capital, takes time to accumulate. You cannot build it in a crisis. You cannot manufacture it when you suddenly need it. You have to invest before you need the return.

Which is why the most common version of the story I hear from women is the most painful one: not that they were excluded from the rooms where opportunities were born, but that they did not realize those rooms existed until they had already missed years of compounding.

Becoming a Connector

There is one more dimension of relationship capital that I want to introduce before we move on, because it represents the highest-leverage position you can occupy in any professional network.

Most people think about relationship capital in a transactional way: who can help me, how do I get access to them, what do I need to do to earn their trust. This is a reasonable starting point, but it describes a relatively passive relationship to the network.

The most powerful version of relationship capital is not about extraction. It is about creation.

When you become the person who connects others, who makes introductions that matter, who thinks proactively about who in your network needs to know whom, you shift from being a node in the network to being its connector. And connectors occupy a structurally unique position: they are simultaneously indispensable to everyone they connect, they build relationship capital with both parties in every introduction they make, and they create a reputation for generosity and vision that compounds faster than almost any other professional asset.

The golf course is a natural environment for becoming a connector. You are in a relaxed, extended social context with multiple people over several hours. The conversation naturally moves through topics that reveal needs, interests, and goals. You are in a position to say, "You should meet my colleague who does exactly that," or "I know someone who solved that problem in a really interesting way," and to make that introduction feel organic rather than calculated.

Every introduction you make is a deposit in your relationship capital account with both parties. And unlike financial accounts, there is no limit on how much you can deposit.

The System You Have Been Missing

Here is what the hidden economy means for you, practically and immediately.

If you are a corporate professional, the hidden economy is the reason your organization's stated promotion criteria are not a reliable map to advancement. The criteria describe what gets you considered. Relationship capital determines whether you get selected. Building it is not optional if you want to close the gap between your performance and your outcomes.

If you are an entrepreneur, the hidden economy is the reason that great products and strong marketing are necessary but not sufficient for business growth. Relationship capital is the distribution network that no advertising budget can replicate. It is the system through which your best clients find you, your best partners recognize you, and your best opportunities emerge before your competitors even know they exist.

In both cases, the solution is the same: stop waiting to be discovered and start investing in the environments where the discovery happens.

The golf course is not the only one of those environments. But it is one of the most powerful, one of the most underutilized by women, and one of the most accessible with the right preparation and the right guide.

The chapters ahead are that guide.

"The people in the room are not there by accident. Neither should you be."

CHAPTER FOUR

The Rooms Where Deals Still Happen

There is a meeting happening right now that will never show up on anyone's calendar.

No invite was sent. No conference room was booked. No agenda was prepared. There is no deck, no follow-up email, no official record that anything of significance occurred. And yet, by the time the day is over, a deal will have moved forward, a partnership will have been seeded, a name will have been mentioned in exactly the right moment to exactly the right person, and an opportunity will have begun its journey toward someone who was present and away from someone who was not.

It is not a critique of how business should work. It is simply a description of how business actually works, has always worked, and will continue to work regardless of how many formal processes, digital platforms, and AI-powered tools we layer on top of it.

The rooms where deals still happen are not rooms at all, most of the time. They are fairways and putting greens. They are the seats around a private dinner table after the formal event has ended. They are the corner of a conference bar where two people who were introduced three years ago finally have ninety minutes to talk without an agenda. They are the charity tournament foursome where a sponsor and a potential partner spend four hours discovering they think about the world the same way.

They are a hunting lodge in South Carolina where a group of executives spend three days in the woods together and come back having made decisions that will not surface publicly for six months. They are client tickets to the home team's game on a Tuesday night in October, seats on the fifty-yard line at the local NFL game, or a suite at a PGA Tour stop like the FedEx St. Jude Championship or the BMW Championship, where the point was never the event itself. They are whatever environment your industry has quietly designated as the place where the real conversations happen, different in every field, consistent in every function.

They are every environment designed, intentionally or accidentally, to do the one thing that no digital tool has yet figured out how to replicate: build genuine human trust over extended, unhurried time.

Why These Environments Work

Ask most professionals where deals get closed, and they will describe a boardroom. A formal pitch. A contract signing.

They are not wrong, exactly. Deals do get closed in those settings. But they are describing the last five percent of the process. The other ninety-five percent, the part where someone decides they want to work with you, trust you, bring you in, recommend you, invest in you, or give you the opportunity at all, that part almost never happens in a formal setting.

Sales professionals have a saying that has circulated in business circles for decades: the fortune is in the follow-up. It is usually meant tactically, call back the prospect, send the second email, do not let the lead go cold. But the deeper truth in that phrase is not about follow-up mechanics. It is about the relationship work that surrounds the formal transaction. The fortune, the real one, is not in the follow-up email. It is in the relationship that makes the follow-up feel welcome rather than intrusive. And that relationship is almost never built in a boardroom.

It happens in the environments I am about to describe, and it happens for reasons that are worth understanding clearly, because once you understand why these environments work, you can use them with intention rather than stumbling into them by accident.

The first reason is time. A formal business meeting lasts thirty minutes to an hour. A golf round lasts four. A private dinner lasts three. A conference retreat lasts two days. In a formal meeting, you have enough time to deliver information. In an extended informal environment, you have enough time to reveal character.

Character is what people are actually evaluating when they decide whether to trust you enough to do business with you. Not your credentials, not your track record, not your pitch deck. Those things get you to the table. Character is what makes someone say yes when they have options.

The second reason is the absence of agenda. In a formal business context, everyone knows why they are there and what is being decided. That awareness creates performance. People manage their words, manage their image, manage the narrative. In an informal environment, particularly one with a shared activity at the center of it, the performance tends to drop. People talk about their families, their frustrations, their genuine interests and ambitions. They reveal themselves. And when people reveal themselves to each other over several hours of shared experience, the trust that forms is qualitatively different from the trust built across a conference table.

The third reason is shared challenge. Whether it is a golf hole that is humbling everyone equally, a cooking class that produces results of varying quality, or a ski slope that makes no distinction between executives, shared challenge levels the hierarchy. The CEO who three-putts the eighteenth green becomes, for a moment, just a person who three-putted the eighteenth green. The founder who asks her playing partner for advice on her grip is not performing vulnerability, she is actually asking for help. These small moments of shared humanity are the raw material of genuine relationships, and they do not emerge in formal settings no matter how skilled the facilitator.

The fourth reason is one that most people sense but have never seen explained in scientific terms, and it is perhaps the most powerful of all.

In 1950, social psychologists Leon Festinger, Stanley Schachter, and Kurt Back conducted a landmark study at MIT's Westgate housing complex, examining friendship formation among students who were strangers to one another. What they found became one of the most replicated findings in social psychology: the single greatest predictor of whether two people became close friends was not shared values, not shared interests, not personality compatibility. It was physical proximity. Students were roughly ten times more likely to form friendships with people who lived in adjacent apartments than with those who lived further down the hall. The people who became friends with residents on multiple floors were almost exclusively the ones who lived next to the stairwells.

Their research gave formal name to something human beings have always instinctively understood: we bond with the people we are near, and we are drawn toward the people we do things with. Subsequent research has built on this foundation consistently. Studies on shared physical activity specifically find that moving, walking, and working alongside another person accelerates the trust-formation process in ways that sitting across from that person never does. Dating coaches have long used this research to advise couples to go on active first dates rather than passive ones, because the brain does not fully distinguish between the bond formed with someone during a shared physical experience and the bond formed over time through accumulated trust. It begins forming the connection regardless.

Researchers call this the propinquity effect. What it means practically is this: four hours walking a golf course beside someone does more for a professional relationship than four months of email exchanges, because your neurology is doing work in that environment that your conscious mind never even registers.

This is not anecdote. This is wiring. And the informal access environments this chapter describes are, whether their designers knew it or not, perfectly engineered to trigger it.

The Geography of Opportunity

Let me name the rooms specifically, because part of what keeps women out of them is that no one ever told them clearly what they are or where to find them.

The golf course is the most powerful of these environments, and the one this book is most concerned with, not because it is the most glamorous but because it is the most consistent. A four-hour golf round provides more uninterrupted, agenda-free time with high-value contacts than almost any other professional activity available. The pace of the game creates natural pauses in conversation, which means nothing feels forced or interrogative. You walk alongside people. You ride alongside people. You wait alongside people. Over four hours, the conversation goes wherever it goes, and it almost always goes somewhere real.

Private dinners and after-event gatherings are the second most powerful environment, and the one most women are already participating in without fully recognizing its strategic value. The formal event, the conference session, the awards ceremony, is rarely where the most important conversations happen. The conversations that matter happen after, when the program has ended, the ties have loosened, and the people who are still there are the ones who wanted to stay. If you leave when the official event ends, you are leaving before the meeting begins.

Charity tournaments occupy a unique category because they combine golf with a social good framework that makes participation feel natural and unguarded. The competitive element creates shared experience. The cause creates common ground. And the format, typically a scramble, which means teams rather than individual competition, creates collaboration rather than rivalry. I have watched more business relationships begin at charity tournaments than at any other single type of event, because the conditions are almost perfectly designed for the kind of relaxed, authentic engagement that produces trust.

Conferences and retreats create a different kind of access: concentrated time with a concentrated group of relevant people. The sessions are not the point. The hallways, the dinners, the early morning runs, the late-night conversations at the bar, those are the point. The professionals who extract the most from conferences are not the ones who attend the most sessions. They are the ones who treat the white space between sessions as the primary event.

I was reminded of this recently when I overheard a fellow entrepreneur respond to a friend's invitation to attend a conference. Her reason for declining: the panel topics didn't interest her. I didn't interject in the moment, but I thought about it for days afterward. Who cares what the panelists are discussing? My target client is going to be in that room. That is the only reason I need to be there: to meet, connect, and build with the people who are already raising their hands to be in the same space as me. The sessions are the wrapper. The relationships are the gift.

Sporting events and client tickets occupy a category that gets almost no attention in conversations about professional access, which is exactly why they deserve attention here. A suite at your local NFL or NBA game, a day at a PGA Tour stop in your market like the FedEx St. Jude Championship in Memphis or the BMW Championship, tickets to the home team on a Wednesday night in February, these are not perks. They are curated relationship environments. The host controls who is in the room.

The shared experience of the game creates instant common ground. The informal energy of a live event, the crowd, the stakes, the unpredictability, produces the kind of relaxed, unguarded conversation that a conference room never will. Client-facing executives at every level use these outings as standard relationship tools, and the point is never the score. It is the three hours alongside someone you need to know better, or someone a client needs to meet, or a prospect who needs to experience what it feels like to be taken care of. If someone in your industry is known for hosting those outings, they are not being generous. They are being strategic. And if you are not yet getting those invitations, it is worth asking yourself why, and who is.

Hunting trips and outdoor retreats represent another access environment that rarely surfaces in business books written for women, which is part of why so many women do not know they exist. In industries like commercial real estate, energy, agriculture, financial services, and parts of the South and Midwest, the annual hunting trip is as embedded in the relationship calendar as any client dinner. These trips run two to four days. They involve shared physical activity, close quarters, and the kind of extended informal time that produces the deepest professional bonds. I am not suggesting you need to hunt. I am suggesting you need to know these trips exist, understand who is on them, and think clearly about whether there is an equivalent experience in your industry that you are currently missing.

Mastermind groups and peer advisory circles are among the most underutilized access environments for women in business, particularly entrepreneurs. These small, ongoing groups of non-competing professionals who meet regularly to share challenges, strategies, and introductions create exactly the kind of sustained, high-trust relationships that generate the most valuable opportunity flow. They are slow to build and extraordinary in return.

The Question Nobody Asks Out Loud

Here is the question I hear underneath every conversation I have with women who are skeptical of this thesis: Is this really still how it works? In 2026, after years of promises about diversity, equity, and inclusion, after remote work was supposed to level the playing field, after LinkedIn and Zoom and every other platform swore they would democratize access, are we really still talking about golf courses and private dinners as the places where business gets done?

Yes. More than ever.

Because here is what happened. The DEI programs that promised to open doors have been systematically dismantled. The corporate initiatives that were supposed to formalize sponsorship and create structured pathways for women have been rolled back, defunded, or quietly eliminated. The safety net that was never fully reliable has been largely removed. And what we are left with is the same system that existed before any of those programs: an informal network of relationships, built in informal environments, by the people who understood that the formal systems were never the real game anyway.

This is not a political statement. It is a practical one. When the structured pathways close, the unstructured ones become more important, not less. When formal inclusion programs disappear, the ability to build relationships directly in the environments where decisions are made becomes the only reliable alternative. The women who built relationship capital before DEI initiatives existed were not waiting for a program to give them access. They were creating it themselves. That strategy did not stop working. It never needed the programs to begin with.

The data is not ambiguous. A 2023 survey by the Golf Industry Association found that 90 percent of Fortune 500 CEOs play golf. A study by the Business Research Company found that the golf industry generates over $84 billion annually in the United States, a significant portion of which is driven by corporate and business-related activity. Harvard Business Review research on professional networks consistently finds that informal relationship environments are where the most consequential professional introductions and opportunities originate, not formal processes.

The rooms have not gone away. They have simply gotten better at appearing not to exist.

What Zoom Cannot Do

I want to address the counterargument directly, because it is a reasonable one and it deserves a real answer rather than a dismissal.

The pandemic accelerated remote work, normalized video calls, and forced many professional relationships to develop entirely in digital environments. Relationships did form. Business did get done. For several years, there was a genuine question about whether the informal physical environment would reassert itself or whether a new model of purely digital professional relationship had emerged.

We now have the answer: physical proximity and shared experience are not optional features of professional trust. They are foundational to it.

This does not mean digital relationships have no value. They do. A relationship that begins in person and is maintained digitally can be strong and productive. But a relationship that begins and exists only digitally has a structural ceiling on the depth of trust it can generate, because trust at its deepest level is built through exactly the kinds of signals that a camera cannot capture.

Body language. The way someone responds under pressure. Whether they treat the server the same way they treat the CEO. How they handle losing. How they handle winning. Whether they are who they say they are when the meeting is over and the stakes are low.

You cannot see any of that on a Zoom call. You can see all of it over four hours on a golf course.

The professionals who understood this came out of the pandemic years with a renewed appreciation for the informal access environment, not a diminished one. Corporate golf participation did not decline post-pandemic. It accelerated. The pent-up demand for the kind of trust that only extended in-person time can build drove a surge in exactly the environments this chapter describes.

The rooms are not a relic of a previous era. They are a response to the limitations of the current one.

The Shella Sylla Test

Early in my banking career, before I understood any of this, I used to measure the quality of a professional relationship by the quality of the business outcomes it produced. Good relationship: they gave me business. Transactional relationship: I had to ask for it every time. Bad relationship: it never went anywhere.

It took me years to understand that I had the causality backward.

The quality of the relationship did not explain the business outcome. The environment in which the relationship was built explained both.

The colleagues who were producing results I could not match, who had pipelines I could not explain, who seemed to receive referrals and introductions as a matter of course while I was grinding for every one, were not better networkers in the formal sense. They were not sending more LinkedIn messages or attending more industry events. They were spending time in different environments. Some of those environments I genuinely did not know about. But if I am being completely honest, some of them I had been invited to and turned down.

I had a blind spot. A significant one.

A female colleague pulled me aside one day and asked me, point blank, why I never accepted invitations to go for drinks after work. My answer was always the same: previous engagement. She looked at me and said, with a very specific kind of sarcasm that only a good colleague can deliver, "Oh right, that's you. You have the BBD. The Bigger Better Deal."

She was not wrong, exactly. But she was also not right. The truth was simpler and more embarrassing than that. I did not like going out after work. When the workday ended, I was tired. I wanted to go home. And most of the time, everyone was drinking, smoking, and talking about work, which was the last thing I wanted to do when work was technically over.

What I did not understand was what was actually happening in those rooms. The conversations that looked like unwinding were actually intelligence gathering. The gossip was organizational insight. The off-hand comments about upcoming projects and leadership decisions were the kind of real-time information that shaped careers. The people staying for drinks were not just socializing. They were, whether they knew it or not, building the kind of informal access that produces outcomes no amount of excellent daytime performance can replicate.

I was missing all of it.

What made it worse was that I did not even have a practical excuse. I did not drink. I did not know how to order a drink. I had never really learned, and walking into a bar setting where everyone had a glass and I had nothing felt uncomfortable in a way I could not fully articulate at the time.

The same colleague who called out my BBD habit decided to do something about it. She hosted an informal gathering at her home. Small group, comfortable setting, the sole purpose of which was to teach me how to order a drink. Not a strong one. Something I would actually like. She made me drinks that evening, let me taste a few options, and made clear that I could spend the night if I was not comfortable driving home. She did not make it a lesson. She made it a gift. I walked away that night with a Malibu Bay Breeze as my go-to drink to order. It is not fancy. It is not a Cosmopolitan or a Jack on the Rocks. But it was mine, and it gave me exactly the start I needed.

I started accepting the after-work invitations after that.

And I started paying attention to what was actually being exchanged in those rooms. The gold I had been leaving on the table was significant. Projects that had been decided informally before they ever hit an official meeting. Promotions that had been discussed in someone's ear before the position was ever posted. Corporate culture signals that explained things I had been misreading for months.

The golf course was the most important of those environments. Not because of the golf, but because of what four hours of shared, unhurried, agenda-free time does to a professional relationship. It accelerates the trust cycle by a factor that is almost impossible to replicate any other way.

When I finally understood this, I did not just start playing golf. I started paying attention to which environments the people I most wanted to know were spending their informal time in, and I found ways to be present in those environments. Golf was the primary one. But it was the principle, not the sport, that changed my results.

The principle is this: if you want to build the kind of relationships that generate the best opportunities, you have to be willing to go where those relationships are actually built.

That is not a compromise with a flawed system. It is a strategic decision about where to invest your time and energy when both are limited and the stakes are high.

Two Types of Professionals

I have spent more than two decades watching professionals navigate these environments, and I have noticed a pattern that holds almost without exception.

There are professionals who attend the golf outing and treat it as an obligation to survive. They arrive, they play, they leave. They are present but not engaged. They are polite but not memorable. They go back to the office and report that they attended the event and nothing came of it.

And there are professionals who attend the same golf outing and treat it as what it actually is: four hours of unstructured, agenda-free time with people who matter to their goals, in an environment specifically designed to produce the kind of candid, relaxed conversation that builds genuine trust.

These two people can play the exact same round, in the same foursome, on the same course. Their outcomes will be nothing alike.

The difference is not confidence. It is not golf skill. It is not personality. It is orientation. One person is trying to get through the event. The other is trying to invest in the relationship. One is measuring success by whether anything visibly transactional happened. The other is measuring success by whether she left knowing the person better than she arrived.

The transactional mindset produces transactional results. The relational mindset produces compounding returns.

This is true on a golf course. It is true at a private dinner. It is true at every opportunity environment you will ever enter.

How you show up in these spaces determines what comes out of them, and that is entirely within your control.

Entering the Room

I will be direct about something that often goes unspoken in conversations about access environments.

For many women, and particularly for women of color, entering these environments is not a simple matter of deciding to show up. These spaces were not designed for us. In some cases, they were explicitly designed to exclude us. The history of women in golf clubs, women in private dining rooms, women at the client outing, is not a history of welcome. It is a history of exclusion that was defended as tradition.

Knowing that history is not a reason to stay out. It is a reason to enter with your eyes open, with your strategy clear, and with the confidence of someone who understands exactly what she is walking into and why.

The rooms did not create the opportunity. The relationships inside them did. The rooms are simply where those relationships were allowed to form. And now that the doors are opening, however slowly, the question is not whether you belong there.

You do.

The question is whether you are prepared to make the most of it when you arrive.

That preparation starts now.

"I stopped waiting to be invited and started making sure I was already there."

CHAPTER FIVE

Why Golf Became the Business Language of Access

Golf did not become the dominant informal environment of American business by accident.

It became that way because a specific group of people, at a specific moment in American economic history, decided that it would be. They built the courses, wrote the rules, established the culture, and then quietly ensured that the people who played together were the people who did business together. The game and the commerce became so thoroughly intertwined that separating them eventually became almost impossible. And by the time anyone thought to ask why the most important professional relationships seemed to form on golf courses, the answer had been baked into the structure of corporate life for so long that it simply felt like the natural order of things.

Understanding how that happened is not just a history lesson. It is the foundation for understanding why the game still works the way it does, why the access gap it created is as consequential as it is, and why learning to navigate it remains one of the most leveraged investments a professional can make.

The Game Before the Business

Golf is old. Versions of it were being played in Scotland by the fifteenth century, and the game spread through Britain and eventually to North America as the British Empire expanded its reach. But golf's emergence as a distinctly American business tool is a product of a much more specific era: the post-World War II economic expansion of the late 1940s through the 1960s.

The postwar American economy was generating wealth at a scale the country had never seen. New industries were emerging and old ones were consolidating around the people who controlled the relationships. The professional class was growing, and with it a new corporate culture built around the idea of the executive as a distinct social type, a person whose work was not physical labor but relationship management, strategy, and decision-making. These men, and they were almost exclusively men, needed environments where they could conduct the informal business of relationship-building. The golf course was perfectly suited.

Private clubs had existed in America since the late nineteenth century, many of them modeled on British institutions, but the postwar period saw an explosion of country club membership among the professional and executive class. By the 1950s, membership in a country club was not simply a leisure choice. It was a professional credential. The relationships formed on those courses were the pipelines through which deals moved, executives were recruited, and the informal power structures of American business were built and maintained.

President Dwight Eisenhower played golf more than eight hundred times during his presidency, and his public love of the game transformed it from a pastime of the wealthy into an aspirational symbol of professional success. The image of the executive on the golf course became, in the 1950s and 1960s, as iconic as the corner office.

What the Game Does That Nothing Else Can

Golf's dominance as a business environment is not a cultural accident. It is a direct result of the game's structural properties, the specific combination of time, physical activity, social rhythm, and psychological conditions that it creates.

No other common professional activity provides four to five uninterrupted hours of time with a small group of people. No other activity combines physical movement, which we now know activates the propinquity effect described in the previous chapter, with the natural conversational rhythms that a golf round produces. The game requires enough focus that you cannot be on your phone or distracted by other business, but not so much focus that conversation is impossible. It creates a shared challenge that everyone in the foursome navigates together, which produces genuine moments of both vulnerability and triumph. It has built-in rituals, the handshake on the first tee that opens the round, the concession of a short putt, the handshake on the last green that closes it, and the nineteenth hole that follows, that create a social script everyone can follow regardless of how well they know each other.

It also has a leveling quality that is unusual in professional environments. A golf handicap means that a scratch golfer and a twenty-handicapper can compete on relatively equal terms. An executive and a client, a senior partner and a junior associate, a vendor and a buyer, can all play together in a format where the competitive stakes are genuine but the hierarchy is temporarily suspended. That suspension, even if it lasts only four hours, creates the conditions for a different kind of conversation than any formal professional context allows.

There is also the matter of character revelation. Golf is one of the few environments where how someone handles adversity, how they respond to a bad break, whether they count their strokes honestly, how they treat the people working the course, is on full display for hours at a time. Experienced business golfers are not just playing the game. They are reading the person.

There are countless stories from executives who made final decisions about hiring, partnering, or investing after a round of golf that confirmed or contradicted everything they had learned about a person in formal settings. The golf course does not lie about character the way a conference room does.

The Exclusion That Was Never Accidental

Here is the part of the history that does not get told in golf's official narrative.

The culture of business golf that emerged in the postwar era was not simply built by men who happened to like the game. It was deliberately constructed to include certain people and exclude others. Private golf clubs in the United States maintained explicit racial exclusion policies well into the twentieth century. Many clubs excluded Jewish members. Virtually all excluded women from full membership, from tee times during peak hours, or from the men's grills and clubhouses where the post-round business conversations happened.

Augusta National Golf Club, home of the Masters and perhaps the most symbolically powerful address in American golf, did not admit its first Black member until 1990 and did not admit women as members until 2012, when former Secretary of State Condoleezza Rice and financier Darla Moore became the club's first two female members on August 20 of that year. These are not ancient history dates. 1990 is within the professional lifetime of most senior executives working today. 2012 is recent enough that many women reading this book were already mid-career when it happened.

The exclusions were not incidental to the business culture that formed around golf. They were structural to it. By controlling who could play, private clubs controlled who could participate in the informal professional relationships that the game facilitated. The golf course was not just a place to play. It was a gatekeeping mechanism for the access economy, one that operated with complete social legitimacy because it was framed as tradition and private association rather than as the economic exclusion it actually was.

The consequence was not simply that women and people of color missed pleasant afternoons on beautiful courses. The consequence was that they were systematically excluded from the relationship environments where careers were accelerated, deals were made, and power was distributed. The access gap in American professional life is not a soft cultural problem. It has a structural origin, and that origin has a specific address.

The Modern Game and Why It Changed

Something started shifting in the 1990s and accelerated significantly in the 2000s and 2010s.

Tiger Woods won the Masters in 1997 with a twelve-stroke margin that remains one of the most dominant performances in major championship history. He was twenty-one years old and Black, playing a sport whose most prestigious venue had admitted its first Black member only seven years earlier. The cultural impact of his dominance was not simply sporting. It democratized the game's image in a way that nothing before it had. Golf went from a sport culturally coded as white and wealthy to a sport with a global superstar whose following cut across every demographic. Participation grew. New audiences engaged.

The emergence of TopGolf in the mid-2000s, with its driving range format and social atmosphere, created an on-ramp for people who were intimidated by the formality and cost of traditional golf. You did not need clubs, a handicap, or a lesson to go to TopGolf. You needed a group of friends and a credit card. The barrier to entry dropped dramatically, and with it some of the social exclusivity that had kept the game inaccessible.

Corporate golf culture also evolved. Companies began explicitly including golf outings in their diversity and inclusion programming, not because the sport had been transformed, but because the business case for having more women and more diverse professionals in those environments had become impossible to ignore. The data on relationship-driven revenue and the cost of exclusion from informal professional networks had accumulated to the point where forward-thinking organizations were actively trying to close the access gap rather than perpetuate it.

None of this means the game became equitable overnight. The exclusions that were built into the culture over a century do not dissolve in two decades. The demographics of golf course membership, tournament leadership, and club governance still reflect the history that shaped them. But the direction of change is real, the pace of change has accelerated, and the window of opportunity for women who understand this moment is wider than it has ever been.

The Language Nobody Taught You

Here is something I want you to sit with.

Business golf has its own language. Not just the terminology of the game itself, the birdies and bogeys and handicaps and preferred lies, but a social language. An unspoken set of norms about pace of play, about etiquette on the course, about how business conversation is and is not introduced during a round, about what happens in the clubhouse after, about the rituals that signal belonging to someone who has been part of this culture for a long time.

Men learn this language the way they learn most professional norms: from other men, informally, starting early. A father teaches a son. A mentor takes a junior colleague out for the first time. A college roommate invites you to his club for the weekend. The knowledge transfers through proximity and relationship over years.

Women, as a general rule, did not receive that education. Not because they were incapable of learning it. Because the people who carried the knowledge were not passing it to them. There is a saying that gets handed down quietly in certain circles: your degree gets you the job, golf gets you the promotion. Fathers say it to sons. Uncles say it to nephews. Nobody says it to daughters and nieces. The language of business golf was transmitted through a network that women were largely excluded from, which meant that even when the formal exclusions began to lift, the informal knowledge gap remained.

This is part of why I built what I built. Not just to teach women how to swing a club, though that is part of it. But to teach women the language of the environment: what to say, what not to say, how to carry yourself, what the etiquette means and why it matters, how to use the round as a relationship-building tool rather than just as a sporting event. The game itself is learnable in weeks. The culture takes longer, and most women have never had anyone willing to teach it to them.

That changes now. The knowledge is yours. Use it.

Why It Still Matters More Than Ever

I am sometimes asked, usually by someone who wants to argue that golf is declining in relevance, whether the game is really still the primary access environment in a world where Pickleball is growing faster, where younger executives are more comfortable with casual social settings, where the country club model feels increasingly dated to a generation that did not grow up with it.

My answer is consistent: the specific activity is not the point. The point is extended, informal, shared time with people who matter to your professional goals, in an environment that produces trust through the mechanisms described in Chapter 4. Golf remains the single most common and most institutionally embedded version of that environment in American professional culture. It is the game that the Fortune 500 CEO plays. It is the outing that the corporate client expects. It is the format that has been standard in industries like finance, real estate, insurance, energy, and professional services for seventy years.

When those industries change their primary relationship-building environments, the advice will change. Until then, the woman who knows how to play, how to carry herself on a course, how to have the right conversation at the right moment during a round, has access to something that her equally talented colleagues who skipped the lesson do not.

That access is not a small advantage. In a competitive professional environment where relationships drive outcomes, it is often the only advantage that matters.

The Moment the Language Opens Up

I have watched this moment happen dozens of times, and it is one of the most satisfying parts of what I do.

A woman decides to learn golf. She is accomplished, confident, successful in every formal professional dimension. She has never played. She may have actively avoided it, dismissed it as a game for people who are not like her, or simply never prioritized it because no one told her what was actually at stake.

She learns the basics. She learns the language. She learns the etiquette and the social rhythms and the specific way that a business golf round works when it is working well. And then she goes out, and she plays, and something happens.

She is in the room.

Not as a visitor. Not as someone who had to be explained or accommodated. As a peer. As someone who speaks the language, understands the culture, and can hold her own in an environment that was not designed for her but that she has decided to inhabit anyway.

The confidence shift is visible. The professional outcomes follow.

This is what access actually looks like when it becomes real. Not a seat at a table. Not a policy or a program. A skill set, a cultural fluency, and the decision to walk through a door that was always technically open but that nobody ever told you how to find.

"The game was never the point. The game was always the door."

CHAPTER SIX

The Gender Gap No One Talks About

I want to ask you something before we go any further.

Think about the five most consequential professional opportunities of your career. The promotion that changed your trajectory. The client that doubled your revenue. The introduction that opened a door you did not even know existed. The partnership that made your business viable. The conversation that led to the board seat, the contract, the round of funding, the role that felt like it was finally the right size for your ambitions.

Now ask yourself: where did those opportunities originate?

If you trace them back honestly, most of them did not start with a job posting or a formal application or an RFP. They started with a conversation. A relationship. Someone who knew you, thought of you, and made a call or an introduction at a moment when it mattered.

Now ask the harder question: who was in the room where that conversation happened?

And who was not?

The Gap That Does Not Show Up in the Data

There is a gender gap in pay that gets measured and published and debated on a regular basis. There is a gender gap in corporate leadership, in venture capital funding, in board representation, in startup valuations, in wealth accumulation. These gaps are documented. They are real. And they are important.

But there is another gender gap that almost never gets named in those conversations, and I believe it is one of the primary mechanisms driving all of the others.

It is the access gap. The gap between the informal environments where professional relationships are built, opportunities are born, and decisions are quietly made, and the professionals who are present in those environments. For most of American corporate and business history, that gap fell almost perfectly along gender lines. The rooms where deals happened were rooms that women were not in.

Not because women were unqualified. Not because women were uninterested. But because the rooms themselves had been constructed, culturally and in many cases literally, to exclude them. The golf course with its restricted tee times and men-only grills. The private club with its male-only membership. The hunting trip that everyone knew was where the real decisions got made, where the invitations went to the men and the women found out what had been decided on Monday morning.

The pay gap, the leadership gap, the funding gap: these are downstream consequences of an upstream problem. The upstream problem is access. And the access problem has an address.

What the Numbers Actually Say

Let me put some numbers to this, because the data is more pointed than most people realize.

Women hold approximately 10 percent of Fortune 500 CEO positions as of 2026, up from essentially zero forty years ago. That progress is real. But consider what it means in practice: nine out of ten of the most powerful corporate positions in America are still held by men. The relationship networks those men belong to, the informal ecosystems they navigate, the golf courses and private clubs and charity tournament foursomes they move through, are still predominantly male by a wide margin.

According to the National Golf Foundation, women represent roughly 25 percent of golfers in the United States. That means the golf course, which the Golf Industry Association tells us is where 90 percent of Fortune 500 CEOs spend relationship-building time, is three-to-one male. In the industries where golf is most embedded, finance, commercial real estate, insurance, energy, professional services, the numbers skew even further.

Women-owned businesses receive less than 3 percent of venture capital funding, a figure that has barely moved in a decade despite enormous attention and intention. The investors making those funding decisions are disproportionately men who know each other, went to school together, sit on the same boards, and play golf together on weekends. The deals that get done first are almost always the deals where someone already has a relationship. And the women who need capital are still, too often, on the outside of those relationship ecosystems looking for a way in.

These numbers are not coincidences. They are consequences. The access gap is not a soft cultural problem. It is a structural economic one, and it compounds over time the same way that relationship capital compounds: quietly, invisibly, and with enormous cumulative effect.

The Cost Nobody Calculates

Here is what I want you to understand about the access gap that I think most conversations about gender equity miss entirely.

It is not just about the opportunities that were lost. It is about the opportunities that were never generated.

Relationship capital, as we explored in Chapter 3, compounds. Relationships produce more relationships. Access to one room opens access to other rooms. A referral leads to a client, who leads to an introduction, who leads to a partnership, who opens a door to an investor or a board seat or a market that would not otherwise have been reachable. The professional who is inside that network does not just get one advantage. They get an ongoing, self-reinforcing flow of opportunity that builds on itself year after year.

The professional who is outside that network does not just miss one opportunity. They miss the entire compounding chain that the opportunity would have started.

Economists have a term for this: network effects. The value of a network grows with each additional connection. But the corollary is also true: exclusion from a network does not just cost you what you would have gotten. It costs you everything that would have compounded from what you would have gotten.

Women who were excluded from business golf networks in 1985 did not just miss a few pleasant Saturdays on a course. They missed thirty-five years of compounding relationship capital. They missed deals and referrals and introductions and partnerships and promotions and board seats and funding rounds and clients that would have been generated by the relationships they were never allowed to build.

That is not a soft cultural harm. That is a structural economic loss. And it is still happening, in real time, to women who are present in the workforce, present in corporate America, present in entrepreneurial ecosystems, but absent from the informal environments where the most consequential professional relationships are being built.

The Pushback I Always Hear

I have been having conversations about this for over twenty years, and I know what some of you are thinking right now. Because I have heard it in every workshop, at every speaking engagement, from accomplished women who bristle at the suggestion that the answer to a structural problem is for them to learn a sport.

It usually sounds something like this:

Why should women have to adapt to a broken system? Why should we have to learn golf to succeed? Why don't we just change the culture instead of assimilating into it?

I understand that response. I felt it myself, early on, when I first understood what was happening. There is something genuinely infuriating about being told that the solution to your exclusion is to become fluent in the language of the people who excluded you.

But I want to offer you the answer I have arrived at after two decades of working in this space, and I want to give it to you straight, the way I would tell it to a woman I genuinely care about, which is how I think of every woman I work with.

The question is not whether the system is broken.

It is.

The data makes the case clearly. According to the Institute for Women's Policy Research, at the current rate of progress, white women will not reach pay parity with white men until 2076. For Latinas, the projected date is 2160. For Black women, 2183. We are not talking about a gap that is closing on a human timescale. We are talking about a structural problem that, without meaningful intervention, will outlast the careers of every woman reading this book, and the careers of their daughters and granddaughters after them.

The question is not whether the culture should change.

It should.

The question is what you are going to do with your career, your business, and your economic future while you are waiting for the culture to catch up. Because the culture has been catching up, slowly and unevenly, for fifty years. And the women who waited for the invitation, who stood at the edge of those rooms and insisted they should not have to learn the language, are still waiting.

I am not interested in waiting. And I do not think you are either.

The Strategic Answer

Here is the distinction I want to draw, because I think it is the most important one in this entire book.

There is a difference between assimilation and strategic fluency.

Assimilation means adopting the values, norms, and identity of a dominant culture in order to be accepted by it. It means becoming less of yourself in order to fit in. It means erasing the parts of your identity that make the gatekeepers uncomfortable, and it often comes at a cost to your integrity, your authenticity, and your sense of self.

Strategic fluency means something entirely different. It means learning how a system operates well enough to navigate it on your own terms. It means understanding the language of an environment so that you can participate in it without abandoning who you are. It means choosing, deliberately and with full awareness of the choice, to enter rooms that were not built for you and to use your presence in those rooms to create the opportunities that should have been available to you all along.

I am not asking you to become someone else. I am asking you to become fluent.

The woman who walks onto a golf course for a corporate outing does not check her values at the clubhouse door. She brings everything she is into that environment. Her intelligence, her relationship skills, her professional instincts, her humor, her character. She does not play golf the way a man plays golf. She plays golf the way she plays golf. And in doing so, she is present in a room where her male peers are building the relationships that drive their businesses, and she is building them too.

That is not assimilation. That is access. And access, in an economy where opportunity flows through relationships, is the most leveraged investment a professional can make.

What Changes When Women Are in the Room

This is the part of the conversation that does not get told often enough, because so much of the narrative around the gender gap focuses on what women have lost. Let me tell you what changes when that equation shifts.

When women are present in informal professional environments, the nature of those environments changes. Not because women are inherently more virtuous or collaborative, though research on gender and leadership style does point to some meaningful differences in approach. But because diversity of perspective in any relationship environment produces diversity of outcome. The deals that get considered expand. The talent that gets discussed expands. The businesses that get funded, the partnerships that get formed, the opportunities that flow through the network expand, because the network itself has expanded.

The companies that have done the most intentional work on closing the access gap, not just the representation gap, have seen measurable returns. McKinsey's research on gender diversity and financial performance has been consistent for years: companies in the top quartile for gender diversity in leadership outperform their peers on profitability and value creation. The mechanism is not simply representation. It is the relationship networks, the client relationships, the market access, the talent pipeline, and the decision-making quality that diverse leadership unlocks.

The business case is not just about fairness. It is about performance. And the access gap is not just a justice issue. It is a value-destruction problem for organizations that have not solved it.

The Woman Who Is Already Behind

I want to speak directly to something that may be sitting with you as you read this.

If you have been in your industry for ten, fifteen, twenty years, and you are only now understanding the full shape of the access gap, you may be feeling something that is hard to name. A kind of retroactive grief, maybe. For the opportunities you did not know you were missing. For the rooms you did not know existed. For the years you spent working harder when you should have been working differently.

That feeling is real, and I am not going to tell you it is not.

But I want you to hold it alongside something else.

The access gap is real. The time you did not spend in those rooms is real. And you cannot recover what compounded for other people while you were not in the network.

What you can do is start compounding now.

Relationship capital, like financial capital, does not care when you begin. It only cares that you begin. The woman who starts building her network intentionally at forty-five is not as far behind as she thinks, because the network she is building now will compound forward. The relationships she forms today will generate opportunities for the next twenty years of her career. The access she gains this year will open doors that will not close.

The best time to start was twenty years ago. The second-best time is today.

The Invitation Nobody Sent

Here is the truth that has stayed with me through twenty years of this work.

Most of the women I work with were never told the rules.

Not because the rules were hidden from them maliciously, though sometimes they were. But because the people who knew the rules assumed that the people who needed to know them were already in the network where the rules got passed down. And women, by design or by default, often were not.

Nobody told you that the golf course was where the real business happened. Nobody told you that the charity tournament foursome was where your male colleague's referral network was built and maintained. Nobody told you that the standing tee time on Thursday afternoon was not just a leisure activity but a relationship maintenance ritual that was driving six figures of business through someone else's pipeline every quarter.

And because nobody told you, you did not know to show up.

It is the conversation that should have happened twenty years ago, told to you now, with everything I have learned from building a career in those environments and then spending the better part of two decades teaching other women how to enter them. You were never behind because you lacked the capability. You were behind because you lacked the information. Now you have it.

"Nobody told us the rules. So we learned them, and then we changed who gets to make them."

CHAPTER SEVEN

What Happens When Women Enter the Game

There is a moment I watch for when I work with women learning to navigate golf as a professional environment. It does not happen on the driving range. It does not happen during the lesson. It happens later, usually a few weeks after someone has gone out for the first time in a real business context, and they come back and try to describe what the experience was like.

They almost always start with what went wrong. The topped drive on the third hole. The lost ball. The approach shot that sailed thirty yards right of where they intended. They catalog the mistakes with a precision that would impress a tour caddie.

And then, usually about halfway through the debrief, something shifts. They stop talking about their swing and start talking about the conversation they had on the seventh fairway. Or the moment when the CFO told them something in the cart that she had never shared in any board meeting. Or the way the whole dynamic of a relationship that had been formal and slightly transactional for two years suddenly became easy and real after four hours of shared struggle on a golf course.

That is the moment I am watching for. The moment the game stops being about the game.

This chapter is about what actually happens when women enter these environments. Not the theory of it. The reality of it. The specific, concrete, sometimes surprising ways that access to informal professional environments changes professional outcomes.

Stacy's Story

Here is the story in full.

Stacy was in her mid-twenties and a year or two into her career at a top recruiting firm in Birmingham, Alabama. She was the kind of professional who makes everything look easy: sharp, quick, competitive, with the kind of instinctive relationship intelligence that is either present or it isn't. She was good and she knew it, which in a young woman reads sometimes as confidence and sometimes as something that makes certain people uncomfortable. In her office, it read as both.

She had identified a role she wanted. A promotion that would have moved her from contributor to manager, the kind of step that changes not just your title but your visibility, your relationships, and your trajectory. She did what she had been told to do: she made her intentions known. She sat down with her boss and told him directly that she was ready for the opportunity and that she wanted to be considered.

Her boss dismissed her. Not harshly, not cruelly, but clearly. The timing wasn't right. She needed more seasoning. There was a vague implication that someday, when certain things aligned, there would be a conversation. But not today.

She went back to her desk and kept working.

The Open Spot

A few weeks later, the firm had a company golf tournament coming up. Her boss had put together a foursome with key prospects, the kind of outing that blended client entertainment with competitive fun, the sort of afternoon where relationships that had been building for months could solidify into something durable over four hours and a shared scoreboard.

One of the colleagues in the foursome had to drop out at the last minute.

Stacy found out about the opening and did not wait to be asked. She walked into her boss's office and said she had played golf in high school and would like to take the open spot.

He agreed. Reluctantly, by her account.

What happened on the course that day is the part of this story that I think reveals something important about why golf works the way it does as a professional environment. Stacy is an excellent golfer. She played competitively in high school, and while she had not played much in the years since, the foundation was there. She was comfortable on the course in a way that her boss, who had probably assumed she would be a liability to his foursome, had not anticipated.

She was not a passenger. She was a competitor.

They played well together. The foursome won the tournament. And in the process of winning, they cemented the relationship with the prospects they were hosting. A client was landed. The outing was, by every professional measure, a success.

A few weeks after the tournament, Stacy was promoted into the exact role she had been told she was not ready for.

What Actually Changed

I want to be precise about this, because I think the easy version of the story, the version that says "she played golf and got promoted," misses the more important lesson.

Nothing changed about Stacy's qualifications between the conversation in her boss's office and the promotion. Her skills were the same. Her track record was the same. Her potential, which her boss had presumably assessed when he told her the timing wasn't right, was objectively unchanged.

What changed was what her boss knew about her. More specifically, what he had seen with his own eyes in an environment where professional performance is not performed. It is revealed.

In a business meeting, you are presenting a version of yourself. You are managing the impression, choosing your words carefully, monitoring the room, calibrating your tone. You are, in the best and most professional sense of the term, on. The golf course does not give you that option for four straight hours. You are walking. You are making decisions under pressure with real consequences, even if the consequences are only a few strokes on a scorecard. You are handling adversity in real time, a bad lie in the rough, a missed putt under the pressure of a close match, and the people around you are watching how you handle it. You are talking, genuinely talking, not pitching or presenting or managing, to people whose opinions of you matter.

Stacy's boss had two years of strong performance reviews to draw on. After the tournament, he had something more valuable: he had watched her compete. He had seen her composure under pressure. He had watched her carry her own weight and more in a high-stakes context where her behavior affected not just her own outcome but the firm's relationship with a real client. He had seen her as a peer.

That is not something a performance review can produce. That is a different kind of evidence.

The Visibility Shift

There is a concept in organizational psychology called attribution. It describes the mental process by which people assign causes to the outcomes they observe. When we watch someone succeed, we attribute that success to either their internal qualities, their skill, their character, their intelligence, or to external circumstances: luck, an easy task, a favorable situation.

One of the most consistent findings in research on gender and the workplace is that women's successes are more likely to be attributed to external factors than men's successes. When a man wins a client, his colleagues tend to think: he is talented and persuasive. When a woman wins a client, her colleagues are more likely to think: the client liked her, or it was an easy pitch, or she got lucky with the timing.

This attribution gap is not always conscious. It is often a completely invisible bias operating beneath the surface of professional judgment. But it has real consequences for who gets promoted, who gets sponsored, and who gets considered when opportunities arise.

Golf disrupts the attribution gap in a specific and powerful way. When you compete on a golf course, the performance is direct and unambiguous. There is no easy client, no favorable situation, no luck that explains a well-played round. You hit the ball or you don't. You make the putt under pressure or you miss it. Your composure in a difficult moment is visible to everyone in the foursome.

Stacy's boss had been, almost certainly without meaning to, attributing her strong performance in the office at least partly to favorable circumstances. Good clients, a helpful team, an easy territory: the usual explanations people reach for when they want to explain away someone else's success. Golf gave him four hours of evidence that was harder to explain away. It is difficult to attribute a well-played competitive round to luck. The skill, the composure, the competitive instinct: those read as internal qualities. Her qualities.

She did not change his mind about her. She gave him new information that changed it for her.

The Pattern Repeats

Stacy's story is a particularly vivid version of something I have watched happen in less dramatic ways dozens of times across the women I coach and work with. The specific details vary. The underlying pattern does not.

Renee was in commercial real estate in the Southeast and had been trying to break into a specific segment of her market for two years. The decision-makers in that segment were a tight-knit group, known to each other, doing business with each other, not actively hostile to outsiders but not naturally inclusive either. She learned the game and started showing up at the industry charity tournaments that drew that community every year.

After the third tournament, one of the senior brokers in that group started introducing her to people. Not because she asked him to. Because she had spent twelve hours over three tournaments as part of the same competitive ecosystem, and at some point, she had simply become someone he knew and trusted rather than someone he recognized but had never really engaged with.

Within a year, she had three new clients from that network. All three came through introductions he made. None of them came through any formal process.

Diane was running her own financial advisory practice and had been struggling for years to build a referral network with estate attorneys, a notoriously relationship-driven professional community that tends to refer business among people they have known for a long time. She learned golf, started playing in a monthly scramble that several local estate attorneys participated in, and within eighteen months had her single strongest referral relationship with an attorney who had become a genuine friend as well as a professional partner.

The attorney had never referred business to a financial advisor he hadn't played golf with. She did not know that when she started playing. She knows it now.

The Pattern Beneath the Stories

What these stories share, what Stacy's story shares with every version of this story I have watched unfold, is not a simple formula. It is not: learn golf, get promoted. That is not how it works. If it were that simple, everyone would do it and the advantage would disappear.

What the stories share is a specific mechanism: the translation of existing capability into visible, legible, trusted competence in an environment that bypasses the filters through which women's professional performance is typically evaluated.

Every woman in these stories was already good at her job before she entered the golf environment. Stacy was already qualified for the promotion. Renee already had the skills to serve those clients. Diane already knew how to build strong client relationships. What they lacked was not capability. It was visibility in the environments where capability gets converted into opportunity.

Golf, and informal professional environments more broadly, serve as translators. They take internal capability and render it visible in a format that decision-makers can assess directly, without the distorting filters of formal performance management, without the attribution biases that operate in formal settings, without the intermediaries and processes that slow down and complicate the way competence moves through organizations.

Four hours on a golf course is a shortcut. Not a shortcut to developing the skill or doing the work. A shortcut to being known and trusted by the people whose decisions shape your professional outcomes.

The Client That Doesn't Come Through a Pitch

I want to address the entrepreneurial reader directly for a moment, because the stories I have shared so far are weighted toward the corporate context. The mechanism is the same in business ownership, but the stakes are sometimes even more immediate.

For an entrepreneur, a client is not a promotion. It is revenue. It is the difference between a business that survives and one that doesn't. And in many industries, particularly in B2B service businesses like professional services, consulting, financial advising, real estate, and construction, the client acquisition process is fundamentally relational. The business goes to the person the buyer trusts, not necessarily the person with the best proposal.

The women I work with who own businesses have shown me something about golf as a business development tool that is slightly different from the corporate use case. In the corporate context, golf is primarily about internal visibility: being seen differently by people who already know you. In the entrepreneurial context, golf is often about external visibility:

being seen at all by people who have never had a reason to consider you.

That deal, the one that doesn't come through a pitch, comes through a relationship. And the relationship has to start somewhere. We will go deeper on what that looks like for entrepreneurs in Chapter 8.

The Changed Dynamic

I want to return to something I mentioned at the beginning of this chapter, the moment I watch for when a woman comes back from her first real business golf experience.

What I see in those conversations is not primarily excitement about golf. What I see is surprise at how much the dynamic shifted.

Professional relationships have a default mode: formal, role-defined, shaped by the titles on either side of the table. There is a buyer and a seller, a boss and a direct report, a client and a vendor, a senior partner and a junior associate. Those roles carry assumptions that are almost impossible to escape inside formal professional settings. They shape how people communicate, what they share, what they withhold, how they make decisions about trust and risk.

Four hours on a golf course suspends those roles. Not permanently. Not even for the whole round. But enough. Enough for something different to become visible. Enough for the person on the other side of the formal relationship to see you as a human being with a sense of humor and composure and genuine competitive spirit rather than as a function you perform within a professional transaction.

That suspension, even temporary, changes things. It creates a foundation for a different kind of relationship, one in which the formal context is no longer the only context, in which there is a reservoir of shared experience and genuine warmth to draw on when the formal stakes are high.

I have watched this happen between a woman entrepreneur and a potential investor who had been cordially uninterested for two years. I have watched it happen between a woman executive and a senior colleague whose support she needed for a major initiative but who had always been slightly remote. I have watched it happen between a woman in sales and a client who had been loyal but not particularly close, and who became, after a charity tournament outing, a genuine champion for her business.

The game changed the dynamic. The dynamic changed the outcome.

You Do Not Have to Be Good to Win

One thing I want to make sure is clear before we leave this chapter, because I have watched the performance anxiety around golf keep talented women out of environments that would have changed their trajectories.

None of the women whose stories are in this chapter were accomplished golfers when the pivotal moments happened. Stacy was a strong golfer, but she was the exception. Most of the women I work with are beginners or high-handicappers who are still working on the fundamentals. Diane was shooting scores in the nineties when the key relationship was built. Renee was losing balls on every other hole in those early tournaments.

It did not matter.

The golf course is not primarily a place where people evaluate your golf game. It is a place where people evaluate your character, your composure, your humanity. A beginner who plays with good etiquette, who handles a bad shot with humor, who genuinely engages with the people she is playing with rather than retreating into self-conscious embarrassment about her score, is a better business golf partner than a scratch golfer who is difficult company for four hours.

The game is not the point. The game is the context.

What you bring to the context is what matters. And what you bring to any context, which is your character, your intelligence, your genuine interest in the people around you, your ability to be fully present: those are not things you need to practice at a driving range. You already have them.

The only thing golf requires of you is that you show up.

"She didn't win the round. She won the room. In business, the room is the only score that matters."

CHAPTER EIGHT

The Deal Flow Advantage

Ask any entrepreneur where her best clients came from, and she will tell you a combination of things.

Word of mouth. Referrals from happy clients who sent someone their way. Visibility through her local chamber of commerce or an industry association she showed up to consistently. A marketing campaign that worked. A conference where she met the right person at the right moment. A relationship she had been tending for two years that finally converted when the timing was right.

This is the honest answer. Most businesses grow through a mix of channels, and the mix varies by industry, by market, and by the individual entrepreneur. There is no single engine.

But when you trace the highest-value clients, the ones who paid the most, stayed the longest, referred the most freely, and generated the most meaningful growth: those almost always lead back to a relationship. Not a transaction. Not a campaign. A person who knew her, trusted her, and put their own credibility behind her name.

That pattern matters. Because it tells us something important about where to invest.

The chamber of commerce works because it creates recurring proximity with the same community of local business people over time. The industry conference works because it puts you in a room with peers and potential clients in an environment designed for connection. The referral works because someone trusted you enough to act on your behalf.

What all of these have in common is relationship capital: access, visibility, and trust that compounds over time and converts into opportunity.

Golf, for the entrepreneur who is not currently playing it, belongs in this same conversation. Not as a replacement for what is already working, but as an addition to it, and in many markets, a significant one.

This is the chapter for the women who are building something. Not climbing someone else's ladder, but constructing their own. And the argument I want to make is not that you should abandon what is generating deal flow today. It is that there is a channel most women entrepreneurs have not yet tapped, one that the men in your market have likely been using for years, and that understanding it could meaningfully change the quality and pace of your growth.

How Business Actually Grows

There is a version of entrepreneurship that gets told in pitch competitions and business school case studies. A founder identifies a problem, builds a solution, acquires customers through scalable marketing channels, raises capital, and grows. The engine of growth in this version is the product and the process.

That version is real. But it describes a small fraction of how most businesses actually grow, and an even smaller fraction of how most women-owned businesses grow given the access gaps that shape where capital and clients actually flow.

The more common version, the one that does not get written up in TechCrunch but that plays out in hundreds of thousands of businesses every year, looks more like this:

A woman builds something genuinely good. She works hard, delivers results, and develops a reputation. Then growth stalls, not because the product is wrong, not because the market is wrong, but because the people with the budget to buy it, the capital to fund it, or the network to refer it do not know she exists, or do not know her well enough to trust her with the opportunity.

The gap is not capability. The gap is proximity.

This is not a motivational observation. It is structural. Research on entrepreneurial networks consistently shows that the primary driver of venture funding, client acquisition at higher price points, and strategic partnership formation is not the quality of the pitch or the strength of the product. It is the strength of the founder's existing network and the degree to which that network includes people with the resources and authority to act.

In other words: who knows you, what they think of you, and whether they think of you when it counts.

That is relationship capital. And for entrepreneurs, it is not a soft skill. It is the engine.

The Referral Nobody Sends Over Email

There are two kinds of referrals in business, and they are not created equal.

The first is the passive referral. Someone mentions your name when asked. They say you're good, pass along your contact information, and leave the rest to you. This is the kind of referral most professionals receive. It is valuable. It is also relatively easy to generate at a certain threshold of performance.

The second is the active referral. Someone does not wait to be asked. They think of you and immediately call the person who needs to know about you. They make the introduction personally, with warmth and specificity. They vouch for you. They stay engaged with the outcome. This is the kind of referral that changes a business.

The difference between the two is almost entirely determined by the depth of the relationship between you and the referral source.

Passive referrals come from people who know your work. Active referrals come from people who know you.

Golf builds the second kind of relationship. Not because there is anything magical about the game itself, but because of what the game requires: four to five hours together, unscheduled and unhurried, with no agenda beyond the round. In that context, conversations go places they do not go in offices. People reveal more of themselves. You learn what someone is actually worried about, what they are proud of, what they are building toward. They learn the same about you. By the end of eighteen holes, even two people who met at the first tee know each other in a way that a dozen thirty-minute phone calls would not produce.

And that kind of knowing is what generates active referrals.

I have watched this play out repeatedly among the women I coach. Women who came to golf wanting to learn the game and discovered that the game was generating the kind of business development they had been trying to manufacture through networking events and social media, and doing it faster and more durably than either.

The Pipeline That Builds Itself

One of the women I work with, Angela, owns a commercial cleaning company in Birmingham. She is excellent at what she does, has a strong reputation among her existing clients, and had spent years trying to expand into a larger corporate account base through conventional means: cold outreach, proposals, referrals from satisfied clients.

Growth was slow. The corporate facilities managers she needed to reach were not responding to cold emails. The referrals she was getting were warm but small.

She started playing golf.

Within eighteen months, she had been paired in charity scrambles with three facilities directors at companies she had been trying to reach for years. She got there intentionally: she identified industry associations that were natural homes for her target clients, including groups focused on hospitality and commercial real estate, and showed up to their events and tournaments consistently. The pairings were not engineered. They were the natural result of being present in the same professional community, repeatedly, over time. Proximity became familiarity. Familiarity became trust. Trust became contracts.

Two of those three facilities directors became clients. The third referred her to someone who became her largest account.

She did not close any of those relationships on the golf course. She built them there. The business conversation happened later, but it happened in the context of an established relationship, which meant it was not a sales conversation. It was a conversation between two people who already trusted each other, which is a completely different dynamic.

That is what I mean when I say golf generates high-trust referrals and high-trust client relationships. The trust is built before the transaction begins. Which means the transaction is smoother, the client is better, and the relationship tends to be more durable.

Why Entrepreneurs Are Leaving Deal Flow on the Table

Here is the honest version of why most women entrepreneurs are not using golf as a business development tool, even when they suspect they should.

Some have been told the game is too expensive, too time-consuming, too male, or too intimidating to be worth the investment. Some believe that as entrepreneurs, they can simply outwork the access gap: if the product is good enough, if the marketing is consistent enough, if the hustle is relentless enough, the clients will come. Some have internalized a version of entrepreneurship that is primarily about building, not relating, and have not fully reckoned with how much of the building depends on the relating.

And some have simply never been shown the connection between the golf course and the pipeline. Nobody told them.

I want to tell you now.

The golf course is not a luxury for your business. It is a business development channel. One of the most efficient ones available, measured in terms of the depth of relationship it produces per hour invested.

The math alone makes the case. A four-hour round of golf, played once a month with clients, prospects, and potential referral partners, represents forty-eight hours of relationship-building time per year in a context specifically designed to accelerate trust. No conference, no networking event, no virtual meeting replicates that quality of time. And unlike most business development activities, golf provides a shared experience, not just a shared conversation, which is what creates the kind of memory and association that makes you the first person someone thinks of when the relevant opportunity arises.

Opportunity Environments: Engineering Your Own

Not every relevant person in your industry plays golf. Not every business development opportunity will flow through the fairway. Part of what the best entrepreneurs understand is that the principle behind golf, spending extended, informal time with the people who matter to your business goals, can be applied to other environments as well.

I call these Opportunity Environments: settings where trust builds naturally, relationships deepen, and opportunities emerge not as the stated purpose of the gathering but as the organic consequence of people who respect each other spending meaningful time together.

Golf is the most reliable Opportunity Environment I know of, because it has built-in structure, duration, and shared challenge that accelerate relationship formation. But a well-designed dinner, a small retreat, a mastermind group, a charity board, a recurring social event with a consistent community of people you respect: all of these can function as Opportunity Environments if they are built and tended with intention.

The women I know who have the most consistently strong deal flow are not the ones who attend the most networking events. They are the ones who have built or joined a small number of high-trust, recurring communities where the same people show up over time, relationships compound, and business flows as a natural consequence of the trust that has been established.

The key word is recurring. A one-time event produces exposure. Recurring presence in the same community produces relationship capital. And relationship capital is what produces deal flow.

What the Accounting Firm Owner Understands

One of my clients, Carol, runs an accounting firm. She is not a golfer herself, but she is one of the sharpest business developers I know, because she understands something that many business owners miss: relationship capital is a team asset, not just a personal one.

She has an employee who plays golf regularly. She does not just tolerate it, she actively supports it. This includes the time it takes during the week, because she has watched what it produces. That employee has developed a healthy and growing pipeline through his golf relationships: prospects who know him, trust him, and think of him first when their accounting needs change or when someone in their network asks for a recommendation.

She has not closed deals directly from a golf course. But she has seen clearly enough what golf does for her employee's relationships, and by extension for her firm's pipeline, that she treats his golf as a business development investment, not a perk.

That is a sophisticated understanding of how deal flow actually works. The pipeline does not always come through you directly. Sometimes it comes through the people around you who are in the right rooms, building the right relationships, on behalf of the business you are both trying to grow.

For the entrepreneur who is not a golfer but leads a team, this is worth sitting with. Who in your organization has the personality, the presence, and the interest to be a genuine relationship builder in the golf community? Supporting that person's access to the game, and to the business community that surrounds it, may be one of the highest-return investments you make in your firm's business development capacity.

Most entrepreneurs understand this intellectually. Fewer act on it consistently, because the return is not immediate. You do not play one round of golf and close a client. You play thirty rounds over three years and discover that your pipeline fills without you having to force it.

That is the compounding effect of relationship capital at work. And the women who learn to build it early, in the right environments with the right people, develop a business development advantage that cannot be replicated by any algorithm, any marketing budget, or any AI-assisted outreach sequence.

The Entrepreneur Who Does Not Have Time

I hear this objection more than any other, from the women I coach and from entrepreneurs in my network who are building businesses while also running households, raising children, managing teams, and doing a hundred other things that compete for the same hours.

I do not have time for golf.

I want to respond to this with both honesty and directness, because the women who say it are usually not wrong about being busy. They are wrong about the calculation.

The question is not whether you have time for golf. The question is whether you have time to not be building the relationships that will generate the clients, partnerships, and referrals your business needs to grow.

Business development is not optional, and it never has been. The only question is how you do it, and how efficiently the time you spend on it converts into the kind of deep, trust-based relationships that produce active referrals and long-term clients.

A four-hour round once a month is twelve to fifteen hours of high-quality relationship time per quarter. That is time that can be structured around people you genuinely want to know better, in a context that is enjoyable and that doubles as leisure and community. Compare that with the same number of hours spent at networking events that produce business cards you never follow up on, or on social media outreach that generates engagement but rarely trust.

Golf is not inefficient. Golf is extremely efficient, if the people you are playing with are the right ones.

The women who have made this shift tell me consistently that it did not feel like adding time to their schedule. It felt like replacing a lower-quality use of time with a higher-quality one, with the added benefit that they were also doing something they came to genuinely love.

Building Your Deal Flow Strategy

I am not going to ask you to become a serious golfer in order to use this chapter. The goal is not par. The goal is proximity to the people who matter to your business, in a context that accelerates trust.

Here is where to start.

First, identify the three to five people in your market whose relationship would most significantly change your business trajectory. Not warm contacts, not friendly acquaintances. The people whose referral, partnership, or endorsement would move the needle. Write down their names.

Second, ask yourself where those people spend their informal professional time. Do they play golf? Do they appear on charity tournament sponsor lists? Are they members of a club? Do they attend a particular conference or serve on a particular board? The answer tells you which Opportunity Environments to prioritize.

Third, get into those environments. This may mean learning to play golf. It may mean joining a board, or attending a conference, or hosting a dinner. The specific vehicle matters less than the principle: be physically present, consistently, in the places where the people you want to know are building their own relationships.

Fourth, invest in the relationships without attaching them to transactions. Be genuinely curious about the people you meet. Follow up. Show up consistently. Become a connector in the community, not just a participant. Make yourself useful. Over time, the business will follow.

I know this sounds slower than running a targeted ad campaign. It is. It is also more durable, more enjoyable, and far more likely to produce the kind of growth that is sustainable.

The women who understand this are not waiting for deal flow to arrive. They are building the conditions under which it becomes inevitable.

"The best pipeline I ever built had nothing to do with marketing. It had everything to do with the people I chose to spend time with."

CHAPTER NINE

AI Changes Everything and Nothing

There is a conversation happening in every industry right now, in board rooms and break rooms, in strategy sessions and over quiet moments of private anxiety, about what artificial intelligence is going to change.

The answer, if you have been paying attention, is: a great deal.

AI is already writing first drafts of legal briefs and marketing copy. It is reading and summarizing financial statements faster than any analyst. It is generating code, diagnosing images, drafting proposals, building models, answering customer service inquiries, and conducting research that used to take weeks in a matter of minutes. The pace of capability development is not slowing. Every month, the list of tasks that AI can do as well as or better than a human grows longer.

This is the "everything" part of the chapter title. The transformation is real, it is large, and anyone who tells you it will not affect your industry or your role is not being straight with you.

But here is the other half of the paradox, the part that gets less attention in the anxious conversation about automation:

The economic decisions that matter most in business, the ones that determine which firms get hired, which leaders get promoted, which deals get done, which partnerships get formed, which investments get made: those decisions are still made by human beings. And human beings, in the final analysis, do not make high-stakes decisions based on data alone. They make them based on trust.

That has not changed. And there is compelling reason to believe it will not.

What AI Actually Automates

To understand why relationship capital becomes more valuable in an AI-saturated economy, it helps to be precise about what AI actually automates and what it does not.

AI is extraordinarily good at tasks that are information-intensive, pattern-based, and high-volume. Processing large amounts of data and identifying patterns. Generating content within established frameworks. Answering questions with retrievable answers. Translating between formats, languages, and levels of complexity. Performing analysis that follows defined rules.

These are not trivial capabilities. They represent a large share of what knowledge workers have been paid to do for decades. And as these capabilities become widely accessible, the economic value of doing them well decreases. Not because the work is less important, but because the work is no longer scarce.

What AI is not good at, what it cannot do in any meaningful sense, is the following:

It cannot build a relationship. It can simulate one, briefly and superficially, but it cannot create the kind of genuine human connection where someone trusts you with their real concerns, their actual budget, their honest hesitation, and their decision-making process. Trust is not given to a system. It is given to a person. And AI cannot read a room: it cannot sense that a negotiation has shifted, that a client is about to walk away for reasons they have not said aloud, that the dynamic in a foursome changed on the twelfth hole and needs to be addressed directly. The social intelligence that lets a skilled professional navigate complex human environments in real time is still entirely human territory.

No AI generates endorsements, because endorsements are acts of personal credibility: they belong to people who have staked something on your behalf. And nothing in any model replaces the experience of being genuinely known. The women in this book who have invested in relationship capital over years find themselves with pipelines that generate without being forced not because they optimized a system, but because they built a community of people who know them as human beings, not as service providers in a database.

These things, the ability to build trust, to read a room, to earn authentic endorsement, and to be genuinely known by the people who matter to your goals: these are the capabilities that AI cannot touch. And they are exactly the capabilities that the Opportunity Environments in this book are designed to develop.

The Scarcity Inversion

Here is the economic logic that I want you to hold onto, because it changes how you think about where to invest your professional development time.

When something becomes abundant, its price falls. When something becomes scarce, its price rises.

For decades, the scarce resources in professional environments were information and analytical capacity. The people who had the most knowledge, the deepest expertise, the sharpest analytical minds: those were the people with the most leverage. Access to information was restricted, analysis was expensive, and the professionals who could do it well commanded a premium.

AI has made information abundant and analysis cheap. The premium on those capabilities has compressed, and it will continue to compress as the technology develops.

What has become scarcer, precisely because so much else is being automated, is genuine human connection. The ability to walk into a room and make people feel known and valued. The kind of relationship where a client calls you before they call anyone else, not because you are the cheapest or the most technically proficient, but because they trust you in a way they do not trust the alternatives. The network that generates opportunity not through algorithms but through people who put their credibility behind your name.

This is the scarcity inversion: as AI makes competence abundant, the scarcest and therefore most valuable professional asset becomes the depth and quality of your human relationships.

The professionals who understood this early, who were already investing in relationship capital before the AI transition accelerated, are not worried about automation. They are insulated from it in the way that matters most: the people who generate their most important opportunities did not hire them for their ability to produce a spreadsheet. They hired them because they trust them as people. And no AI changes that.

The Industries Where This Matters Most

The scarcity inversion plays out differently across different industries and roles, and it is worth being specific.

The roles most exposed to AI displacement are those where the primary value delivered is information processing, pattern recognition, or content generation. Data analysts whose primary output is reports. Paralegals whose primary task is document review. Junior consultants whose primary contribution is research and slide production. Marketing professionals whose primary output is content at volume.

This is not a prediction that these roles disappear entirely. It is an observation that the headcount required to do these tasks is shrinking, and the individuals who remain will need to offer something beyond the task itself.

The roles least exposed to AI displacement are those where the primary value delivered is trust, judgment, and relationship. Examples of these are: senior client management, business development, leadership, and strategic advisory work. Any role where the outcome depends not just on what you know or can produce, but on whether the client, partner, or decision-maker trusts you enough to act on your recommendation.

Notice what this means for the trajectory of a professional career. The early career, the years spent developing technical competence and building a track record, is increasingly the portion most exposed to AI pressure. The later career, the portion that depends on relationships, judgment, and earned credibility, is increasingly the protected portion.

This means the smartest investment you can make right now, whether you are early in your career or mid-career and watching the landscape shift, is to accelerate the development of the capabilities that belong to the protected portion. Build relationships before you need them. Develop the kind of credibility that comes from being known as a person, not just as a performer. Get into the Opportunity Environments where the people who will matter to the next phase of your career or business are building their own relationships.

The window to do this before the transition fully reshapes your industry is not infinite.

The Trust Premium

I want to give this a name, because naming it makes it easier to build toward intentionally.

The Trust Premium is the additional value you command in any professional transaction because of the depth of relationship you have with the decision-maker. It is the reason a client pays your rate rather than a competitor's lower one. The reason a partner chooses you over a more credentialed alternative. The reason a referral source thinks of you first. The reason a door opens for you that is not open for equally qualified people who are not in the room.

The Trust Premium does not show up on a resume. It does not appear in a credentials comparison or a proposal evaluation. It is invisible in formal processes and decisive in informal ones.

And here is what matters about it in the context of AI: the Trust Premium is the one form of professional advantage that automation cannot compress. AI can produce a better first draft, a faster analysis, or a more comprehensive research summary. It cannot produce the feeling in a client's mind that you are the person they trust with this.

That feeling is built over time, in person, through the accumulation of experiences that demonstrate who you are when the stakes are real and the agenda is off. On a golf course. At a dinner where the conversation went somewhere unexpected. In a charity tournament where you showed up and competed and laughed and handled a bad hole with grace. In the kind of environment where you cannot hide behind a polished presentation because there is no presentation. There is just you.

The professionals who are building the Trust Premium now, in relationship environments before the full weight of AI pressure arrives in their industries, are making an investment with a return that compounds in exactly the direction the market is moving.

The Mistake Smart People Are Making

I work with and around a lot of talented, driven women who understand the AI transition intellectually but are responding to it in a way that I believe is strategically backwards.

They are investing more time in developing technical skills to keep pace with automation. Learning new software, acquiring new certifications, expanding their technical toolkit. These are not bad investments. Some of them are necessary. But they are investments in the portion of professional value that is most exposed to AI pressure, doubling down on the capabilities that are being commoditized.

What they are not doing, or not doing nearly enough of, is investing in the portion of professional value that AI cannot touch.

They are not making time for the golf round that would put them in a foursome with the three people who could change the next five years of their career or business. They are not joining the board or the club or the mastermind group that would put them in consistent, recurring proximity with the community that generates their most important opportunities. They are not showing up in the Opportunity Environments where the Trust Premium gets built, because those environments feel like luxuries compared to the urgent work of staying technically current.

The urgency is backwards. Technical currency has a shorter shelf life than ever and a lower premium than ever. Relationship capital has a longer horizon and is appreciating in value, not depreciating.

I am not suggesting you stop developing technical skills. I am suggesting that if you are allocating your professional development time primarily to technical skills and little to none of it to relationship-building environments, you are optimizing for the wrong variable at exactly the wrong moment.

What Has Not Changed

Something gets lost in conversations about disruption and transformation, and it is worth naming before we leave this chapter.

The fundamental mechanics of how human trust works have not changed. They are not going to change.

Trust is built through time, through consistency, and through the accumulation of small interactions that demonstrate character, competence, and genuine interest in the other person. Through shared experiences that reveal who you are when no one is managing the optics. Through the sense, developed over repeated contact, that this person is someone I can count on.

These mechanics were true before AI. They were true before the internet, before the telephone, before the railroad. They are embedded in how human beings are wired to evaluate other human beings, and no technology has ever fundamentally altered them.

What technology does is shift where those interactions happen and who has access to the environments in which trust is built. The golf course, the private club, the charity tournament, the business dinner: these environments are not artifacts of a pre-digital economy. They are expressions of a permanent human need to know the people we do business with as something more than a digital profile or a professional credential.

The professionals who understand this, who have built their strategies around the permanent reality of human trust rather than the temporary reality of any particular technological moment, are the ones who will navigate the AI transition with the most clarity and the least anxiety.

Not because they are ignoring the change. But because they have invested in the thing the change cannot touch.

"AI will make competence cheap. It will never make trust common. Build the thing that cannot be automated."

CHAPTER TEN

How to Enter the Rooms

Everything before this chapter has been the why.

Why the rooms where deals still happen are real, and still operating, and still determining outcomes that formal processes will never fully explain. Why golf became the language of business access, and why that has not changed despite everything else that has. Why women's exclusion from these environments was never accidental and has cost us more than most people have been willing to calculate. Why relationship capital compounds. Why AI, rather than making these rooms obsolete, is making them more valuable. Why the deal flow, the promotion, the partnership, the client that changes your business: these things still find their origins in informal environments where trust is built between human beings who have chosen to spend time together.

You understand the why. Now we get to the how.

This chapter is the one you share with a friend who just got invited on her first business golf outing and does not know where to start. It is the one you come back to before your first charity scramble. It is the one that turns the abstract argument of this book into something you can act on before the end of the week.

And it starts with a story I have been waiting to tell you fully.

The Golf Emergency

She had been putting it off for years.

She was Michelle, a tech executive at a Silicon Valley firm, one of a small number of Black women in her company's senior leadership, smart, accomplished, genuinely excellent at her job. She had heard me make the case for golf more than once. She had nodded in the way that people nod when they agree with something in principle but have no immediate plans to act on it. Someday, she thought.

Then the Regions Tradition came to Birmingham.

Her company had arranged for a significant potential client to come into town for the tournament. A small group of their executives was scheduled to host a round with this prospect, the kind of outing where the relationship work that precedes a major contract gets done. Two weeks before the event, one of the men scheduled to play got called away unexpectedly. She was told she needed to take his place.

She had never played a round of golf in her life. She had no clubs. She had no golf attire. She had two weeks.

Michelle called me in what I can only describe as a state of controlled panic. And I will confess that I allowed myself one small moment of satisfaction before I got to work. I had been encouraging her to learn golf for years. I told her so, briefly and with some warmth, and then I put it aside. There was no time for told-you-so. There was work to do.

Over the next ten days, we did everything.

We went to the driving range. I gave her a crash course in the fundamental mechanics of the swing, not to make her good, but to give her enough to function. I was not trying to build a golfer in ten days. I was trying to build someone who could step onto a course with confidence and handle herself without embarrassment.

We went to purchase clubs. Not top-of-the-line equipment, but a proper set that fit her and that she could swing consistently. The equipment matters more than most beginners realize, because the right clubs give you a chance of making solid contact, and solid contact gives you a chance of feeling capable rather than humiliated.

We went to find an appropriate golf outfit. This is not a trivial detail. Presentation on a golf course signals whether you belong there. Golf has a dress code culture, and showing up in the wrong attire is a distraction you do not need on top of learning the game in two weeks. Confidence starts before you swing a single club. When you look the part, you carry yourself differently.

We went to the golf course and played nine holes together. Not to practice the swing, though that helped too. To give her the experience of being on a course: the rhythm, the pacing, the etiquette, the unwritten rules that experienced golfers navigate automatically and that beginners violate unknowingly. How to mark your ball. When to pick up. How to handle a lost ball without slowing the group. How to tend the flagstick. How to behave at the nineteenth hole after the round is over.

And I gave her the two pieces of advice that I consider the most important things any beginner can bring onto a business golf course.

The first: tell your playing partners upfront that you are a beginner. Not as an apology. Not as a disclaimer. Simply as a statement of fact that sets the expectation and moves on. "I'm still learning the game" is all you need to say. You say it once, at the first tee, and then you never mention it again. You do not apologize for bad shots. You do not over-explain your score. You say it once, set the expectation, and compete.

The second: do not let anyone tell you what club to use.

This sounds like a small thing. It is not. Golf is a sport where experienced players sometimes offer advice to beginners, not always helpfully, and where the advice often comes with an implied social pressure to defer to someone who knows more. A beginner who defers on club selection loses control of her own game and, more importantly, signals that she is someone who can be directed. That is not the signal you want to send in a business context.

I told her what to say if someone offered unsolicited advice about her club choice. She was to look them in the eye and say, calmly and without apology: "My golf instructor has advised me to follow this approach until my game develops." Period. No further explanation. No defensiveness. Just quiet, confident ownership of her process.

By the time the outing arrived, she was not a golfer. She was something more useful for that particular day: she was prepared.

She stepped onto the first tee knowing what to expect, knowing how to carry herself, knowing what to say and what not to say, knowing how to stay engaged even on holes where her shots were not where she wanted them. She was present. She was confident. She was, in every way that mattered that day, in the room.

She held her own.

Michelle had not even made it to her car after the round when her phone rang. It was the colleague whose spot she had taken, calling from across the country. He had already heard from someone at the outing.

"I hear you're quite the prolific golfer," he said.

Shortly thereafter, she received a thirty thousand dollar raise.

The golf did not get her the raise. Let me be clear about that. Her performance, her relationships, her professional track record got her the raise. What the golf did was put her in the room where the people who could make that decision saw her as a whole person, not just a title. It gave them four hours of experience with her that no meeting, no email, no performance review could have provided. It changed what they knew about her and how they thought about her.

That is what entering the room does. The room does not hand you the outcome. It gives you the conditions under which the outcome becomes possible.

What Her Story Actually Teaches

I want to stay with this story for a moment before we move into the practical guidance, because there are several lessons embedded in it that are easy to miss if you take the headline at face value.

The first lesson is that preparation is not the same as expertise. She was not an accomplished golfer on the day of that outing. She was a prepared beginner. And in a business golf context, a prepared beginner who knows the etiquette, carries herself with composure, and stays engaged with the people she is playing with is infinitely more valuable to herself and to everyone in the foursome than an anxious expert who is so focused on her swing that she misses the conversation.

The second lesson is that the moment you enter the room is not when the business happens. It is when the relationship deepens to the point where business becomes possible. She did not close anything on the golf course. She became someone those people knew in a different and more complete way. The raise was the consequence of years of good work that finally had the visibility it needed.

The third lesson is the one I want you to carry most directly into your own situation: the invitation does not wait for you to be ready. It arrives on its own schedule, with its own timeline, and the only question is whether you have invested enough in advance to say yes with confidence, or whether you will be scrambling to catch up when it does.

She scrambled and survived because she had two weeks and a coach and the determination to make it work. Not everyone gets two weeks. Some invitations arrive with less notice. Some arrive in markets where the golf community is tighter and the expectations are higher.

The time to learn the game is before you need it.

Before You Get to the Course

Let me address something directly, because it comes up in almost every conversation I have with women who are new to golf in a business context.

You do not need to be good.

I want to say that again, because the fear of being bad at something in front of professional peers is one of the most powerful barriers keeping women out of these environments, and it is based on a misunderstanding of what business golf actually evaluates.

Nobody in a business foursome is keeping a scorecard of your professional value. They are not thinking less of you because you hit a ball into the rough or needed three shots to reach a green that they reached in two. What they are noticing, what actually matters in a business context, is how you carry yourself. Whether you are present and engaged. Whether you are good company for four hours. Whether you handle the inevitable frustrations of the game with grace rather than drama. Whether you are someone they want to spend time with again.

Those are the variables that determine whether a business golf round strengthens a relationship or weakens one. None of them require a handicap.

What you do need, before you step onto a course in a business context, is a baseline of preparation. Not expertise, but foundation.

The Practical Foundation

Here is what I recommend for any woman who is preparing to enter the business golf environment for the first time, or who wants to show up more confidently in it.

**Take lessons before you take an invitation.* A few sessions with a teaching professional will give you the basic mechanics of a swing that functions, an understanding of how to move through a hole, and enough confidence to step onto a course without feeling completely lost. You do not need to be tournament-ready. You need to be functional. Six to eight lessons will get most beginners to functional.

**Learn the etiquette before you learn the swing.* This surprises people, but the etiquette of golf matters more in a business context than the quality of your shots. Pace of play: keeping up with the group in front of you and not slowing the group behind. Cart and course care: repairing divots, replacing sand, not driving where you should not. Silence during someone's swing. The sequence of who plays when. The way a hole ends and how you move to the next one. These are the things that signal to experienced players whether you belong on the course, and they are entirely learnable without any athletic ability whatsoever.

**Know the basic vocabulary.* Par, birdie, bogey, handicap, stroke play, scramble format. You do not need to be fluent in golf terminology. You need to be able to follow a conversation without looking confused. A short amount of reading will handle this.

**Invest in appropriate equipment and attire.* You do not need expensive clubs. You need a starter set that fits you and that a golf professional has confirmed is appropriate for your build and swing. And you need to dress the part: collared shirt or golf-appropriate top, golf shorts, skirt, or pants, golf shoes if possible. Every club has a dress code and every business outing reflects on everyone in the group. The investment is modest and the return is that you walk onto the first tee looking like you belong there.

**Play nine holes before you play eighteen in a group.* If you have the opportunity to get onto a course before your first business outing, take it. Even once. The difference between understanding golf theoretically and having the physical experience of a full hole, including all the decision-making, the walking, the pacing, the rhythm, is significant. You will show up to your first business round with a different quality of confidence if you have already walked a course.

On the Course: What Actually Matters

You are in the foursome. The round has started. Here is what I want you to focus on.

**The first tee is where you set the tone.* Introduce yourself if you have not met everyone. State simply that you are still developing your game if you are a beginner. Smile. Be warm. Golf foursomes, especially in a scramble format, have a social rhythm that establishes itself quickly on the first tee, and your job is to contribute positively to that rhythm from the start.

Engage with the people, not just the game. The golf is the context, not the point. The point is four hours of relaxed, shared experience with people who matter to your professional goals. Ask questions. Listen. Be curious about who they are beyond their title. The conversations that build relationships happen between shots, on the cart, walking the fairway, waiting for the green to clear. Be present for those conversations rather than lost in anxiety about your next shot.

Handle bad shots with grace and move on. Every golfer, at every level, hits bad shots. What distinguishes the people who are good to play with from the people who are not is not their score. It is how they handle adversity. A brief acknowledgment, sometimes a self-deprecating comment if it fits naturally, and then complete focus on the next shot. Drama over a bad shot, extended frustration, visible deflation: these are the things that make a foursome heavy. Be the person who keeps the energy light.

Do not offer unsolicited swing advice. This is the corollary to not accepting it. Golf is a sport where advice flows freely among experienced players, but it is almost never welcome from someone you have just met, and it can come across as presumptuous or condescending even when it is well-intentioned. Unless someone specifically asks for your feedback, stay focused on your own game and on the conversation.

The nineteenth hole is where relationships close. The conversation over drinks or a meal after the round is not an afterthought. It is often where the most important parts of the relationship get built. The round has broken the ice, established shared experience, and created a natural foundation. The nineteenth hole is where that foundation gets built on. Do not skip it. Do not rush through it. Be present.

When You Are Not Ready for Golf

Golf is the most powerful Opportunity Environment I know of, and it is the one this book has spent the most time on, for good reason. But it is not the only door.

If you are not yet in a position to play golf in a business context, whether because you have not had the chance to learn, because it is not the primary environment in your market, or because you are building toward it, there are other Opportunity Environments worth investing in right now.

Charity boards and nonprofit committees put you in recurring, meaningful contact with community leaders across industries. The relationships formed in the context of shared purpose tend to be particularly durable because they are grounded in values rather than transactions.

Industry association leadership, not just membership but active participation in committees or boards, creates consistent visibility with the most engaged people in your field. The people who show up consistently for association work are often the people who are most invested in their industry's community, which makes them valuable nodes in any professional network.

Private dinners and curated gatherings, hosted or attended, create the kind of intimate, unhurried conversation that conferences rarely produce. A dinner for eight people who are genuinely interesting to each other generates more relationship capital per hour than almost any other format.

And golf itself, even before you are ready to play in a business context, can be accessed through charity scrambles, where beginner-friendly formats and relaxed atmospheres make the game genuinely welcoming, and through driving range outings, which are increasingly social events that do not require any course skill at all.

The principle is always the same: find the environments where the people who matter to your goals are building their relationships, and show up there consistently, over time, with genuine presence and genuine interest in the people around you.

The rooms are open. The question is simply whether you are willing to walk in.

"The invitation is not the hard part. The hard part is being ready when it arrives. Start getting ready now."

CHAPTER ELEVEN

From Participant to Power Player

Getting into the room is not the finish line.

It is the starting line.

This is the mistake I see most often among women who have done the hard work of accessing the Opportunity Environments in this book: they show up, they play the round, they attend the dinner, they join the board, they participate genuinely and leave feeling good about the experience. And then they go back to their regular lives and wait for something to happen.

Nothing happens.

Not because they did anything wrong. Because access is not the same as leverage. Being present is not the same as being strategic. The room opens the door. What you do after the room is what determines whether that door leads anywhere.

This chapter is about the after. The follow-through, the cultivation, the deliberate conversion of a good experience into a durable relationship into a professional outcome. It is about moving from someone who attends the right events to someone who is indispensable in the right community. From participant to power player.

There are two tracks through this chapter, one for the corporate professional building influence inside an organization, and one for the entrepreneur building a business and a market presence. The strategies overlap significantly, but the specific applications differ enough that I want to address each one directly. Read the one that fits your situation now. Read the other one anyway, because most careers eventually include both.

The Follow-Through Is the Strategy

Before we split into the two tracks, I want to establish a principle that applies to both.

The most common failure mode in relationship building is not bad execution in the room. It is failing to execute after you leave the room.

You play a great round of golf with someone. The conversation was warm. There was genuine connection. You exchanged contact information. And then three weeks pass, and neither of you has reached out, and the relationship has not advanced because relationships do not advance on their own. They require tending.

This is not a character flaw. It is a structural problem. Professional life is busy, follow-up feels awkward if too much time has passed, and the urgency of the immediate always crowds out the importance of the long-term.

Sales professionals have been saying it for decades: the fortune is in the follow-up. But as we established in Chapter 4, the deeper truth is not about tactics. The professionals who convert access into leverage solve this with a simple discipline: they follow up within forty-eight hours of every meaningful encounter, without exception, and they do it with specificity.

Not a generic "great to meet you" email. Something that demonstrates you were actually paying attention. A reference to something specific that was said: "I've been thinking about what you mentioned on the back nine about the challenges with your supply chain. I know someone who worked through a similar problem and came out well. Would an introduction be useful?" Or simply: "I really enjoyed the round on Saturday. The conversation on the seventh hole has stayed with me. I'd love to continue it over coffee sometime."

The specificity is what makes the difference. Generic follow-up signals that the interaction was pleasant but unremarkable. Specific follow-up signals that you were genuinely present, that you cared enough to remember, and that you are someone worth knowing better.

That signal is the beginning of everything that follows.

The Corporate Track: Building Influence From the Inside

For the woman building influence inside an organization, the strategic question after getting into the room is: how do I convert this access into visibility, sponsorship, and the kind of relationship capital that moves a career forward?

The answer has several components.

Make yourself known to the people who matter, not just the people you work with directly. One of the most consistent patterns in how women's careers stall is that their strongest advocates are the people immediately around them: their direct manager, their team, their project partners. These are valuable relationships. But they are often not the people with the authority and the reach to move careers.

The informal environments in this book, the golf courses and charity tournaments and conference dinners, put you in proximity to people several levels above your immediate circle. That proximity is only valuable if you use it to build genuine relationships, not to be seen standing next to someone important, but to become someone that person actually knows and thinks about.

This requires follow-through. It requires showing up consistently in the environments where those relationships are built. And it requires patience: the kind of relationship that generates real sponsorship is not built in a single round. It is built over multiple encounters over time, each one deepening the connection.

Understand the difference between a mentor and a sponsor, and pursue both deliberately A mentor gives you advice. A sponsor gives you opportunity. Both are valuable, but they are not the same, and the scarcity of sponsors relative to mentors is one of the most significant structural disadvantages women face in corporate advancement.

A mentor helps you develop. A sponsor advocates for you in rooms you are not in, puts your name forward for opportunities you do not know about, and uses their own credibility to open doors that would otherwise remain closed. Research on professional advancement is consistent on this point: the single most reliable predictor of whether a talented professional advances is not their performance rating. It is whether they have a sponsor.

Golf and other Opportunity Environments are among the most reliable ways to build sponsor relationships, precisely because they create the kind of extended, informal contact where a senior leader gets to see you as a complete person rather than as a subordinate. You cannot manufacture a sponsor relationship from a thirty-minute one-on-one. You can build one organically over eighteen holes.

Once you have those relationships, tend them. Check in. Send the article that is relevant to what they mentioned they were working on. Attend the events they are involved in. Show up consistently. Be someone who is easy and pleasant to think about, not someone who only appears when you need something.

Become the connector in your organization's informal network. We introduced the connector concept in Chapter 3, and I want to bring it back here in a specifically corporate context because it is one of the highest-leverage positions available to someone building influence inside an organization.

When you are the person who makes introductions, who thinks proactively about who needs to know whom, who hosts the informal gathering that brings together people from different parts of the business: you become structurally indispensable in a way that no job description captures. You are the node through which relationships flow. That position builds relationship capital with everyone you connect with, creates visibility across the organization that would be impossible to achieve through normal channels, and generates a reputation for generosity and vision that sponsors notice and remember.

Start small. Host a small lunch for colleagues from different departments who you think would benefit from knowing each other. Make the introduction at the conference that you know both parties need. Bring the junior colleague whose work you admire into the conversation with the senior leader who would benefit from knowing her. Every one of these acts is a deposit in your relationship capital account with multiple people simultaneously.

Manage your visibility with the same intentionality you bring to your performance Most women manage their performance carefully and their visibility accidentally. This is backwards.

Your performance is the foundation. It needs to be strong, and for most of the women reading this book, it already is. What is not strong, in most cases, is the visibility of that performance among the people whose judgment shapes career trajectories.

Visibility is not self-promotion in the uncomfortable sense. It is making sure the right people have accurate information about what you are doing and what you are capable of. It is volunteering for the cross-functional project that puts you in front of senior leadership. It is speaking up in the meeting where it matters rather than saving your analysis for the email afterward. It is accepting the invitation to present at the conference rather than declining because you are not sure you are ready.

And it is showing up, consistently, in the informal environments where leaders form their impressions of people.

The relationship that forms on a golf course is not separate from your professional reputation. It is part of it.

The Entrepreneur Track: Building a Market Position

For the entrepreneur, the strategic question after getting into the room is different: how do I convert access and goodwill into clients, referrals, partnerships, and the kind of market position that makes deal flow sustainable?

The principles overlap with the corporate track, but the application is distinctly different because the entrepreneur is not navigating an internal hierarchy. She is building an external market presence, and the people she needs to cultivate are not above her in an org chart. They are the clients, referral sources, partners, and community leaders who will collectively determine the trajectory of her business.

Build your referral architecture deliberately. Most entrepreneurs receive referrals reactively: a client tells a friend, the friend reaches out. This is valuable but unpredictable. The entrepreneurs with the strongest deal flow have built a referral architecture deliberately, which means they have identified the specific categories of people most likely to encounter their ideal clients and have invested in those relationships with intention.

For a financial advisor, the referral architecture might include estate attorneys, CPAs, and divorce attorneys. For a commercial cleaning company, it might include commercial real estate brokers, property managers, and facilities directors. For a business coach, it might include executive recruiters, HR leaders, and entrepreneurs who serve the same market.

Golf and other Opportunity Environments are particularly efficient for building these referral architectures because the community of business people who golf tends to cut across industries. In a foursome, you might be paired with a banker, a developer, and an attorney: three of the most productive referral relationships for almost any professional services business.

The discipline is the same as the corporate track: follow up with specificity, stay in contact, make introductions that benefit others, and invest in the relationship before you need the referral.

**Host your own Opportunity Environments.* This is the move that separates the professionals who participate in networks from the ones who control them.

When you host, you choose the guest list. You set the context. You are the person through whom all the relationships in the room flow, which means you become the connector by definition. Every relationship formed at an event you host is a relationship that runs through you, and that structural position compounds over time.

This does not need to be elaborate. A quarterly dinner for eight people you want to know better and want to introduce to each other. An annual golf outing for your top clients and two prospects you would like to convert. A monthly coffee for the women entrepreneurs in your community who you respect and want to support. The format matters less than the consistency and the quality of the people you bring together.

The entrepreneurs I know who have the strongest networks are almost all hosts. They create the environments rather than waiting to be invited into them. This is one of the most transferable pieces of advice in this book, and one of the most underused.

Use golf specifically to break into tight professional communities. Almost every market has professional communities that are highly interconnected and difficult to enter from the outside: the commercial real estate broker network, the estate planning attorney circle, the private equity community, the large family business community in any mid-size city. These communities are not closed by formal rule. They are closed by relationship density: everyone in them already knows everyone else, and outsiders are evaluated carefully before being admitted.

Golf, particularly charity tournament golf, is one of the most reliable ways to enter these communities. The charity circuit is by nature open: you register, you pay the entry fee, you show up, and you are in a foursome with whoever you are paired with. And in most markets, the charity golf community is precisely the community you are trying to enter: business owners, senior executives, professional service providers, and community leaders who have been showing up to the same events for years.

The entry is not the challenge. The consistency is. One tournament appearance generates exposure. Ten tournament appearances over three years, at the same events, with many of the same people, generates the familiarity and trust that converts to relationship capital. Show up, play well enough to be pleasant to play with, follow up afterward, and keep showing up. The community will open.

Know when to convert and when to continue investing. This is the judgment call that distinguishes the most effective relationship builders from the ones who either never close or close too aggressively.

The moment to bring business into a relationship is not on the golf course. It is not at the dinner. It is after the relationship has developed enough that the business conversation is a natural extension of the trust that already exists, not an interruption of it.

How do you know when that moment has arrived? In my experience, it is when the other person starts asking you about your business with genuine curiosity, rather than polite interest. When they volunteer information about their own needs or challenges in your area of expertise. When they make an introduction on your behalf without being asked. These are signals that the relationship has matured to the point where business is welcome.

Until then, invest. Show up. Follow up. Connect them to people they should know. Be genuinely useful without keeping score. The conversion will come, and it will be better, more durable, and more likely to generate additional referrals than any conversion that was forced before the relationship was ready.

Becoming the Person Who Creates the Rooms

The highest-leverage position available in any professional community is the one most people never think to pursue.

There are people who attend the rooms where deals happen. There are people who are invited into the rooms. And there are people who create the rooms.

The people who create the rooms, who host the dinners, organize the tournaments, convene the boards, and build the communities where the most important relationships in a market are formed: those people have a structural advantage that is nearly impossible to replicate any other way. Every relationship in every room they create runs through them. Every introduction made at their event strengthens their own relationship with both parties. Every person who meets someone valuable at their gathering associates that value with them.

This is not a position that requires a title or a large platform. It requires consistency, generosity, and a genuine interest in connecting people who should know each other.

SisterGolf was built on exactly this principle. It is not simply a golf instruction program. It is an Opportunity Environment at scale: a community where women who are building careers and businesses come into regular contact with each other and with the broader business community in a context specifically designed to accelerate trust and generate opportunity. Every member who finds a client, closes a deal, or gets a promotion through a relationship built in the SisterGolf community is a return on the investment of creating the environment.

You do not need to build SisterGolf. You need to build something, at whatever scale is right for your market and your goals. A community of ten people who meet monthly. A golf outing that becomes an annual tradition. A dinner series that becomes the event people look forward to. A board you join that you eventually shape.

The point is this: stop waiting to be invited into the rooms. Start building them.

The woman who builds the room is never wondering whether she is in the right place. She is the right place. Every opportunity that flows through her community flows through her. Every relationship that forms in her environment strengthens her position at the center of it.

That is the power player position. And it is entirely available to you.

"Stop waiting for a seat at the table. Set the table. Invite the people who matter. Let the conversation begin."

CHAPTER TWELVE

The Future of Opportunity

I want to take you back to where this book began.

A woman in Miami, early in her banking career, doing everything she was told would work. Preparing harder. Delivering more. Staying later. Hitting the numbers. Waiting, with the patience of someone who had been raised to believe that excellence was its own argument, for the recognition that was supposed to follow.

It did not follow. Not the way she expected. Not on the timeline she had earned.

And then a colleague, over lunch, said something that changed everything. Not because it was complicated. Because it was simple, and true, and nobody had ever said it to her before.

The real business is happening on the golf course. And you are not there.

That woman was me. And the twenty-plus years that followed that conversation have been, in large part, my attempt to make sure that no woman has to wait as long as I did to hear what he told me. That no woman has to spend years pressing her face against glass, watching the rooms where her career and her business are being decided, without knowing the rooms exist or how to enter them.

This book has been that conversation. The one nobody had with you. The one I am having with you now, as directly as I know how.

What We Have Built Together

The argument this book has made is not complicated. The ladder is disappearing. Competence is being commoditized. The rooms where deals still happen are more consequential than ever, and most women are still not in them, not because they lack the capability, but because nobody told them the rooms existed or how to find the door. Relationship capital is the asset that compounds when everything else is being automated. And the women who build it now, deliberately and consistently, in the right environments with the right people, will be the ones who are still standing when the transition completes.

I have lived every part of this. I am not standing outside the argument looking in. I built SisterGolf because I needed what it offers, and because I watched too many women spend too many years doing everything right inside the wrong system. That changes now. It changes with you.

The Decade That Is Coming

I want to be direct with you about what I believe the next decade holds, because the choices you make now about where to invest your professional development time will compound, in one direction or another, for years.

The AI transition is not finished. It is early. The disruption to knowledge work that we have seen so far is the beginning of a longer transformation, and the industries and roles that feel stable today will look different in five years than they do now. The professionals who will navigate this transition most successfully are not the ones who are most technically current. They are the ones who have built the deepest and most durable human relationships in their markets.

At the same time, the rollback of formal DEI structures and corporate diversity programs that we have watched accelerate in recent years means that the informal network has become more important, not less, as a driver of opportunity for women. The safety nets that were never fully reliable have been further weakened. The formal pathways that were supposed to supplement the informal ones have been narrowed. What remains, as it has always remained at the foundation of professional life, is the quality of your relationships and the strength of your position in the communities that generate opportunity.

This is not a moment for discouragement. It is a moment for clarity.

The women who understand that the informal network is the real game, and who are building their relationship capital deliberately and consistently in the right environments, are not disadvantaged by the loss of formal DEI structures. They have built something that does not depend on those structures. They have built the kind of presence and credibility and community that generates opportunity organically, because the people who matter to their goals know them, trust them, and think of them first.

That is a position of genuine power. And it is available to every woman who decides to build it.

What I Want for You

I have spent more than two decades building SisterGolf because I believe, with complete conviction, that access to the right environments changes lives. I have watched it happen. I have seen women walk onto a golf course for the first time, uncomfortable and uncertain, and walk off the eighteenth green with something they did not have before: the knowledge that they belong in these rooms, and the beginning of the relationships that will prove it.

I want that for you.

Not the golf specifically, though I hope you will give the game a genuine chance. I want the access for you. I want the visibility for you. I want the kind of relationship capital that means your name is the first one that comes to mind when the right opportunity opens. I want you to be in the room where your future is being discussed, not waiting outside it.

I want you to stop waiting for formal processes that were never designed with you in mind to deliver what only your own network can, and start building the informal connections that have always been the real engine of professional outcomes.

I want you to understand, in the deepest possible way, that your exclusion from these environments was never about your capability. It was about access. And access is something you can change.

The Women Who Come After You

There is one more thing I want to say, and it is the thing I care about most.

Every woman who enters these environments changes them. Not always dramatically, not always immediately, but persistently and cumulatively in ways that matter.

When you show up at the charity tournament, you make it easier for the next woman to show up. When you join the club, you create a precedent. When you sit at the table where decisions are made, you change what the table looks like and what kinds of decisions it makes. When you build an Opportunity Environment and fill it with women who are building careers and businesses, you are doing something that extends far beyond your own goals: you are creating the access that the next generation of women will inherit.

This is what SisterGolf has always been about at its deepest level. Not golf. Not networking in the conventional sense. The deliberate, persistent work of changing who is in the rooms where the future is decided.

Every member of the SisterGolf community who succeeds, who lands the client, who gets the promotion, who closes the deal, who builds the business: she is not just a success story. She is evidence that the rooms can be entered, the networks can be built, and the access gap can be closed. She is proof of concept for every woman who comes after her.

I want you to be that proof of concept. I want you to be in the room, and I want you to hold the door open behind you.

The Swing That Matters Most

Golf has a concept that I have always found useful beyond the game itself.

In a full swing, the moment of impact, the fraction of a second when the club meets the ball, is over before you are consciously aware of it. Everything that determines where that ball goes has already happened: the setup, the grip, the stance, the backswing, the transition, the path of the club through the hitting zone. By the time of impact, the outcome is already set.

The professionals who struggle most with golf are the ones who focus on the impact. The ones who try to steer the ball at the last moment, who tighten up when it matters most, who make adjustments they cannot make at the speed the swing requires.

The professionals who play their best golf are the ones who trust the preparation. Who set up correctly, execute the swing they have practiced, and let the contact happen as a natural consequence of everything that came before it.

Careers and businesses work the same way.

The opportunities that define your professional life, the promotion that changes your trajectory, the client that transforms your business, the partnership that opens the market you have been trying to reach: by the time those opportunities arrive, the outcome is largely determined by the preparation that preceded them. The relationships you have built. The communities you have invested in. The trust you have accumulated with the people who are in a position to act.

You cannot manufacture that trust in the moment. You cannot build that network when the opportunity is already at the door. The only time to build it is before you need it.

This is the message I most want to leave you with. Not a tactic. Not a technique. A posture toward your professional life:

Invest in your relationship capital now, before you need it, in the environments where it compounds most efficiently, with the consistency and the generosity that makes you someone worth knowing and advocating for.

Set up correctly. Execute the swing. Trust the preparation.

And when the opportunity arrives, as it will, you will be ready.

One Last Thing

When I played in my first charity golf tournament, I was the only woman in a field of a hundred men. I played terribly. I lost balls. I made mistakes that experienced golfers do not make. I am sure there were moments when someone in my foursome wondered why I was there.

But I was there.

And by the end of the round, I had made connections with some of the most significant referral relationships of my banking career. Not because I played well. Because I showed up. Because I stayed in the game. Because I was present in a room that most people in my position had decided was not for them, and I refused to accept that conclusion.

That tournament changed the direction of my career. SisterGolf came ten years later, but it started there, on a golf course in Miami, a young Black woman in a field of a hundred men, playing terribly and connecting beautifully.

The rooms where deals still happen are not waiting for you to be perfect. They are waiting for you to arrive.

So arrive.

Thank you for reading. If this book has changed how you think about where opportunity lives and how to reach it, share it with a woman who needs to hear it. The rooms get better when more of us are in them.

"The rooms were never closed. We just weren't told where the doors were. Now you know. Walk through."

References

Introduction and Chapter One

McKinsey & Company. "The Economic Potential of Generative AI." McKinsey

Global Institute, June 2023. (cited for estimate that generative AI could automate up to 70 percent of tasks currently performed by knowledge workers)

Chapter Two

Granovetter, Mark. "The Strength of Weak Ties." American Journal of Sociology 78, no. 6 (1973): 1360--1380. (foundational research on professional mobility through networks rather than formal processes)

LinkedIn. "The Hidden Job Market." LinkedIn Talent Solutions, 2017. (cited for statistic that up to 70 percent of jobs are filled through networking)

McKinsey & Company and LeanIn.Org. Women in the Workplace. Annual report, published each year 2015--present. www.womenintheworkplace.com. (cited for data that women are held to higher performance standards than men for equivalent roles yet advance more slowly)

Chapter Four

Festinger, Leon, Stanley Schachter, and Kurt Back. Social Pressures in

Informal Groups: A Study of Human Factors in Housing. New York: Harper,

1950. (cited for propinquity effect research at MIT's Westgate housing

complex)

Chapter Five

Golf Industry Association / National Golf Foundation. "Golf

Participation Report." National Golf Foundation, 2023. (cited for

statistic that 90 percent of Fortune 500 CEOs play golf)

Business Research Company. "Golf Courses and Country Clubs Global Market

Report." 2023. (cited for statistic that the golf industry generates

over $84 billion annually in the United States)

Chapter Six

Institute for Women's Policy Research. "Equal Pay in 2025: Gender Gaps

Increased Forecast for Achieving Pay Equity Bleaker." IWPR, December

2025.

https://iwpr.org/equal-pay-in-2025-gender-gaps-increased-forecast-for-achieving-pay-equity-bleaker/.

(cited for projections that white women will not reach pay parity with

white men until 2076; Latinas until 2160; Black women until 2183)

National Golf Foundation. "Golf Participation in the U.S." National Golf Foundation, 2023. (cited for statistic that women represent approximately 25 percent of golfers in the United States)

PitchBook / National Venture Capital Association. "Venture Monitor." Annual report. (cited for statistic that women-owned businesses receive less than 3 percent of venture capital funding)

McKinsey & Company. "Diversity Wins: How Inclusion Matters." McKinsey & Company, May 2020. (cited for data on companies in the top quartile for gender diversity outperforming peers on profitability and value creation)

Chapter Seven

Heilman, Madeline E. "Gender Stereotypes and Workplace Bias." Research in Organizational Behavior 32 (2012): 113--135. (cited for research on attribution gap: women's successes are more likely attributed to external factors than men's)

Chapter Nine

McKinsey & Company. "The Economic Potential of Generative AI." McKinsey Global Institute, June 2023. (cited for analysis of AI automation impact on knowledge work tasks and roles)

www.ingramcontent.com/pod-product-compliance
Lightning Source LLC
LaVergne TN
LVHW010101110826
845155LV00028B/434

* 9 7 8 1 9 5 3 6 5 3 1 9 2 *